SHAKESPEARE ONCE A PRINTER & BOOKBINDER.

FIRST EDITION

Issue limited to 450 Copies.

William Shakespeare, in early manhood, from the bust formerly
in the writer's collection.

Sculptured in marble by F. Hartner.

MAYENCE.

ON THE RHINE

From an Original Drawing by S Prout

Birthplace of Typography.

Type-printing by John Gutenberg began here between 1440 and 1450.

His Latin Bible, the first dated book, appeared in 1455.

SHAKESPEARE ONCE A PRINTER AND BOOKMAN

Lecture One of the Twelfth Series of Printing Trade Lectures
At STATIONERS' HALL, LONDON, E.C.
FRIDAY, TWENTIETH OCTOBER
MCMXXXIII

By

CAPT. W. JAGGARD

With four illustrations

on Nippon vellum

and

Five hundred supporting quotations.

Chairman
SIDNEY HODGSON, Esq.

HASKELL HOUSE PUBLISHERS Ltd.
Publishers of Scarce Scholarly Books
NEW YORK, N.Y. 10012
1972

HASKELL HOUSE PUBLISHERS Ltd.

Publishers of Scarce Scholarly Books

280 LAFAYETTE STREET

NEW YORK. N. Y. 10012

Library of Congress Cataloging in Publication Data

Jaggard, William, 1868-1947.
    Shakespeare once a printer and bookman.

    Reprint of the 1934 ed.
    1. Shakespeare, William, 1564-1616--Knowledge
--Printing. I. Title.
PR3036.J3 1972   822.3'3   70-181003
ISBN 0-8383-1372-8

Printed in the United States of America

SHAKESPEARE ONCE A PRINTER AND BOOKMAN

AN UNWRITTEN CHAPTER

PROSPERO.—All dedicated to . . . the bettering of my mind . . .—*The Tempest*, i, 2.

For it is a chronicle of day by day,
Not a relation for a breakfast.—*The Tempest*, v, 1.

SIR NATHANIEL.—Sir, your reasons have been sharp and sententious.
—*Love's Labours Lost*, v, 1.

A Lecture given in Stationers' Hall, Friday, 20th October, 1933
by
CAPT. W. JAGGARD

THE CHAIRMAN, in introducing the lecturer, said those present were very fortunate in having Captain Jaggard as their lecturer. The name of Jaggard was one which was reverenced by all lovers of, and more especially by students of, Shakespeare, because it was a name which appeared on the title of the First Folio edition of Shakespeare which was printed in 1623. A copy of the facsimile of that Folio edition was in the Hall of the Stationers' Company; the Company could not afford to have the genuine First Folio, as it was worth about £10,000; but they had the facsimile to which he had referred, and there could be seen the name of the printers and publishers, which included Isaac and William Jaggard. Captain Jaggard had been for many years engaged in work in connection with Shakespeare; he lived at Stratford-on-Avon; he had published a Shakespeare Bibliography which was an outstanding work; and, incidentally, he was a Liveryman of the Stationers' Company. The subject of that night's lecture had struck him

(the Chairman) as a little unusual until he had happened a few days ago to have come across a small book by William Blades, entitled "Shakespeare and Typography; being an attempt to show Shakespeare's personal connection with, and technical knowledge of, the Art of Printing," published in 1872, which showed that the idea had been thought of previously; by way of controversy, Mr. Blades suggested that various people had maintained that Shakespeare was doctor, lawyer, soldier, sailor, Catholic, atheist and thief. On the present occasion the audience were going to hear Captain Jaggard argue that Shakespeare was a printer.

CAPTAIN W. JAGGARD then delivered his lecture as follows :—

Since 1623, when William and Isaac Jaggard gave the world its first precious edition of Shakespeare, much ink has passed through the press. Many thousands of editions of our poet have been born. To most of them is prefixed a "life" or sketch of his career. These brief biographies are generally monotonous in their sameness and plagiarism. Nearly all

I

base their outline on the scanty materials gathered by Thomas Betterton the actor, first printed by Nicholas Rowe in his 1709 edition. Likewise, all of them, conveniently for themselves, leave a blank, or unwritten, chapter, covering an entire decade of the poet's life. Those ten vital years, between his ill-considered marriage in 1582 and the appearance of his earliest play, about 1591 or 1592, provide the keynote to his subsequent career and fame. By design, or accident, he drifted into the business affording facility and material for fuller education and psychic development. That secured, the rest was easy, given a mentality such as his.

The object of this address is to probe the mystery of that hiatus, or blank chapter, and to offer a reasonable hypothesis. Any credit for the discovery that Shakespeare once worked as a printer goes to our great trade benefactor, William Blades, author of the "Life of Caxton," and donor of that superb Printers' Library at St. Bride's, standing like an Eddystone Lighthouse over the uncharted rocks of Fleet Street. I propose to go a step further than Blades, and say that our poet was for several years both printer and bookman, for reasons that will presently be apparent. That unwritten, though romantic, chapter in Shakespeare's life-story piques curiosity, and tempts conjecture. There is little direct, but much indirect, evidence. That he was ever one of the unemployed can certainly be rejected. A stripling of twenty-one years, gifted with boundless energy and imagination, could not easily remain idle. Burdened already with wife and three infant children; handicapped by need of income; faced with the downward course of his father's business, is it any wonder

that this depressing outlook directed his wits and vision, and steps toward London? That city of throbbing life offered at least some chanceful opportunity for any worker with ideas. Already he knew that an older school-fellow had taken the same risky step and prospered. This one-time school-chum, now a London citizen, was Richard Field, elder son of Henry Field, a Stratford-on-Avon tanner. So well and truly did Dick Field progress, in this walled city of a hundred miles away, that he sent word home for his younger brother Jasper to come and join him in the printing trade. As most of us know, Dick Field left Warwickshire in 1579, and apprenticed himself for the space of seven years to George Bishop. By an odd arrangement then prevalent, Bishop transferred this new youth for six of those years to another printer, a foreigner, by name Thomas Vautrollier, Huguenot fugitive of France, who took out Letters of Denization on 9th March, 1562. Vautrollier was a scholar, skilful printer, bookseller and binder. His good taste is evident in the founts he employed, while his press-work speaks for itself. Dick Field then was lucky to train under such auspices. In July, 1587, Vautrollier died. Within twelve months Dick Field married his widow Jacqueline, or "Jaklin," and thus, at one stroke, secured a wife and, incidentally, one of the leading London businesses. In 1592, Henry Field, tanner, died at Stratford-on-Avon, and it is significant that in neighbourly friendship, John Shakespeare, the poet's father, was called in to value Field's goods and chattels for probate.

It was towards the end of Dick Field's apprenticeship in 1585, that our poet received information which prompted him to leave his birth-town for a time and stake his little all on the gamble. Scarcely would he be in a position at that time to own a horse. This revolutionary move then meant a weary daily tramp of twenty-five miles, for four days running, to cover the distance. Arrived in the city, he was assured of food and shelter with Dick Field, until work could be found. Thus far we are on sure ground. The rest is deduction based upon ample circumstantial evidence. No doubt exists that at this point Shakespeare was poor; in fact, desperately hard up, with no means in view for maintaining a family of five. It is palpable no cash was available for buying books. Yet books of all kinds, plenty of them, were imperative for the growth and development of his intellect at this juncture. While rural life and the changing seasons had yielded an intimate and wide knowledge of Mother Nature, it was London and London alone that could endow the master-mind with its future cyclopaedic grasp of human psychology; social progress; of court life and statesmanship; of ceremony, pomp, and circumstance; of church, law, medicine, music, arms, and the professions; of oversea travel and customs; of maritime discovery and adventure; of magic, witchcraft, and the occult; of murders, poisons, and crime; in a word, of the whole gamut of mental activity, reasoning, emotion, sentiment, and humour. By and through that mountain of knowledge acquired, our poet was the first British author to use a vocabulary of over sixteen thousand differing words, and likewise, the first Englishman to show the full possibilities of the language, as a vehicle of expression.

To gain this huge store of learning, books were essential to Shakespeare as working tools are to the artisan. There were no such buildings as public libraries until the middle of the nineteenth century. Compared with present-day cost, books were expensive. Second-hand bookshops and subscription libraries did not exist until centuries later. A little free "browsing" might surreptitiously occur at the numerous book-stalls fringing St. Paul's Churchyard, but that "sampling" would not carry one far in scanty spare time. Yet we know full well that Shakespeare read, and read omnivorously, all the best books of the period. But how?

In my "Shakespeare Bibliography, 1911," I described and located some hundreds of volumes we know the poet once used or possessed. Foremost amongst these stand Sir Thomas North's translation of Plutarch, and Raphael Holinshed's Chronicles. Plutarch's "Lives of the noble Grecians and Romans" appeared in six different folio editions, from the press of Richard Field, between 1579 and 1612. This great source-book provided a treasure-house of information about ancient days, couched in stately and sonorous English. It eventually provided plots, materials, or characters, for our poet's classical plays, such as "Antony and Cleopatra; Coriolanus; Julius Caesar; Pericles; Timon of Athens; Titus Andronicus; Troilus and Cressida."

Holinshed's "Chronicles of England, Scotlande, and Irelande" first appeared in 1577, but a fresh and more complete edition proceeded from the press of Henry Denham in 1586-87, in three large folio volumes. This great literary labour played a very important part in our poet's career and writings. Composition had just begun, or was about to start, in 1585, when he reached London, looking for a job. There seems no room for doubt that this huge task, filling two thousand seven hundred and sixteen pages, double columns, supplied in two senses just what he most needed: food for the body, and nutriment for the mind. As a proof reader in Denham's office this folio work would afford him about two years' steady task. In spare time he would assist in Field's office and thus get practical experience of the "art and mystery of printing." In Paternoster Row, at Denham's workshop, he would become friendly with an apprentice there, destined later to play no small part in promoting our poet's fame throughout the world. I refer to William Jaggard, saviour and sponsor of all the known surviving manuscripts of Shakespeare in 1623. This William Jaggard was bound to Henry Denham for a period of eight years, dating from Michaelmas 1584. He was admitted to the Stationers' Company Freedom on 6th December, 1591. With the aid of Dick Field and William Jaggard our poetic youth, fresh from Warwickshire, would quickly become acquainted with city sights and sounds, and with printing processes then in vogue. Afterwards, in 1590-91, Shakespeare would be able to render William Jaggard useful aid at his new business in Fleet Street in proof reading and bookselling.

Running through our poet's forty plays and poems is a stream of technical words and phrases used in printing circles alone. They leave no room for hesitation in concluding that this indeed is the true and only possible explanation of how Shakespeare obtained support for himself and family. It alone unfolds and makes intelligible the means by which he attained consummate knowledge, in after days,

used with such effect in his plays and poems. Can we not picture him at his desk, first in Denham's office, then in Field's shop, and finally in William and John Jaggard's shops in Fleet Street, reading proofs, checking "revises," or selling books? Beside this daily connection with paper and print, our poet stands accused of many other things. As I pointed out in my "Shakespeare Bibliography" various books, pamphlets and articles have been written and published attempting to show that he was, among a hundred odd things:

Actor	Euphuist
Actor's trainer	Falconer
Alchemist	Farmer
Amanuensis	Financier
American	Freemason
Anatomist	Genius
Angler	Gentleman
Archer	Golfer
Armiger	Groom of Royal
Astrologer	Chamber
Astronomer	Historian
Atheist	Horse-holder
Bible student	Horseman
Book-lover	Ignoramus
Botanist	Illiterate
Buddhist	Impresa inventor
Business-man	Industrious
Butcher	Insomnia martyr
Celt	Jester
Chemist	Ladies' man
Christian	Landowner
Churchman	Law-case witness
Cipherist	Lawyer
Courtier	Litigant
Critic	Lover of justice
De Vere, Earl of	Musician
Oxford	Myth
Doctor	Naturalist
Dog-hater	Non-christian
Drunkard	Ornithologist
Emblematist	Patriot
Entomologist	Physician
Ethnologist	Physiologist

Plagiarist
Playhouse manager
Poacher
Printer
Prophet
Protestant
Psychologist
Puritan
Recusant
Romanist
Sailor
Scholar
Schoolmaster
Scotsman
Seaman
Seer
Shapleigh
Sheep-shearer
Singer
Sir Anthony Sherley
Sir Francis Bacon
Sir Walter Ralegh
Skewer-sharpener

Soldier
Sophist
Sorcerer
Sportsman
Statesman
Stoic
Street arab
Superstitious
Surgeon
Swordsman
Temperate
Theatre owner
Tithe owner
Tory
Traveller
Usher (school)
Welshman
Whig
Wiseacre
Wit
Wool-man
Zoologist

As though that load of nick-names was not enough, I have now added another appellation—that of "Bookman."

There is no need to deny many of the designations. Some are so obviously jokes; while many flatly contradict each other. Nearly half of the ascriptions are too preposterous to merit discussion. The fact is, a genius so unique, all-embracing, and yet, withal, so elusive in personality excites curiosity, and guesses are apt to usurp the functions of patient thought and research. So, in short, Shakespeare becomes "all things to all men." That he was, by nature, shy, sensitive, and reticent, goes without saying.

To digress for a moment. Why were his plays and poems not gathered and issued during his lifetime? One reason advanced is: that if folk could read the dramas by their own fireside, they would not trouble or pay to see them performed. A second equally-foolish reason given is that our poet was so weary of correcting other authors' proofs, that he shrank from doing his own. A precedent for publishing a folio volume of plays had already been set by Ben Jonson, who entered his first series at Stationers' Hall, 20th January, 1615, and dated it 1616. But this was only three months ere Shakespeare's death. Tradition says that when he retired home from London, about 1609-10, it was his intention to edit and prepare for press all his writings, and that illness and death overtook him before completion.

It is a pity idle guessers fail to realize that Shakespeare wrote plays for performance, not for print. Each new drama from his pen passed by purchase into the private ownership of the Globe Theatre Limited, in which he was a partner. If the plays were published, there was nothing to stop rival dramatic companies procuring and acting them on tour, to the detriment of the owners. No such thing as authors' "royalties" had yet been thought of.

Let us examine the numerous clues to Shakespeare's familiarity with type-case, press, and bookstore. As Dr. Bucknill pithily says: "Technical expressions are the trade-marks of the mind." William Blades observes: "Nature endows no man (or infant) with ready-made knowledge. A quick apprehension may go far towards making the true lover of nature a Botanist, Entomologist, or Zoologist. The society of Men of Law, Medicine, or Music, may with help of a good memory, store a man's mind with professional phraseology, yet the opportunity of learning must be there. No argument is required to prove that, however highly endowed with genius or imagination, no one could evolve, from his inner consciousness, the terms, customs, or working implements of a trade with which he was unacquainted. If then we find Shakespeare's mind familiar with the technicalities of so peculiar an art as printing—an art which, in his day, had no connecting links with the needs and daily pleasures of the common people as now—if we find him adopting its terms, and referring often to its customs, our claims to call him a printer stand upon a firmer base than those of the divine, doctor, lawyer, or soldier. Our grounds then are strong for inviting thoughtful attention to certain quotations and deductions, which, if not conclusive, yet afford indubitable evidence of his having become practically acquainted with the details of a printing office."

Would Shakespeare, or any contemporary of his, have used trade expressions, technical words, or noted workshop habits, singular to and known only by a very small portion of the community, in plays intended for the general public? While familiar enough to the writer, they would sound strange and mystical to the everyday audience. Shakespeare was too artistic, too wise, to commit so glaring a blunder. With the most charming unconsciousness his technical phrases are often penned unintentionally. His constant care for an ever-fresh vocabulary, or avoidance of threadbare terms, leads him to adopt any simile fitting and suitable to the occasion. When we meet then in his text with some printing-office phrase it is so neatly amalgamated with its context that, although some other expression would have been chosen, had not Shakespeare once been a printer, the ordinary reader or listener is not surprised by any apparent incongruity.

In Tudor days, it must be remembered, the printing and publishing trade was not divided up into so many "watertight" compartments as now. For example, William Jaggard combined the arts of author, printer, engraver, binder, and publisher, all under one roof. On his premises in Barbican one could watch the evolution of an illustrated book, from the virgin white sheet to the finished product.

Now follows an annotated alphabet, derived from Shakespeare's forty plays and poems, containing expressions connected with paper and print. In other words illustrating Shakespeare's daily intimacy with the threefold sister-arts of authorship, production, and distribution of literature. My assemblage of evidence for this purpose is representative, not exhaustive. Enough is quoted to prove how rich and varied are our poet's writings in literary metaphor and simile, stored in his capacious mind since his early days in the combined printing and book trade.

These quotations number nearly five hundred.

ALPHABET OF TERMS

ABSTRACT

Bertram.—Dispatched sixteen businesses, a month's length apiece, by an Abstract of success.—*All's Well*, iv, 3.

Octavius Caesar.—You shall find there a man who is the Abstract of all faults.—*Antony and Cleopatra*, i, 4.

King Philip.—This little Abstract doth contain that large, which died . . . and the hand of time shall draw this brief into as huge a volume.—*King John*, ii, 1.

Duchess of York.—

Brief Abstracts and record of tedious days
Rest thy unrest on England's lawful earth.
—*King Richard III*, iv, 4.

Mrs. Ford.—Neither press, coffer, chest . . . but he hath an Abstract for the remembrance of such places.—*Merry Wives*, iv, 2.

ALMANAC

Enobarbus.—They are greater storms and tempests than Almanacs can report.—*Antony and Cleopatra*, i, 2.

> Note this lapse on our poet's part. The story of the play happened long before the birth of printing in Europe.

Antipholus.—Here comes the Almanac of my true date.—*Comedy of Errors*, i, 2.

Prince Henry.—What says the Almanac to that?—*2 King Henry IV*, ii, 4.

Bottom.—A Calendar! Look in the Almanac! —*Midsummer Night's Dream*, iii, 1

See also—CALENDAR.

ALPHABET

Malvolio.—What should that Alphabetical position portend?—*Twelfth Night*, ii, 5.

See also—CONTENTS, INDEX.

APOSTROPHE

Holofernes.—You find not the Apostrophes, and so miss the accent! Let me supervise! —*Love's Labours*, iv, 2.

APRON

John Holland.—The nobility think scorn to go in leather Aprons.—*1 King Henry VI*, iv, 2.

Bawd.—He will line your Apron with gold. —*Pericles*, iv, 6.

ARISTOTLE

Tranio.—Or so devote to Aristotle's checks, as Ovid be an outcast quite abjured.—*Taming of Shrew*, i, 1.

Hector.—Not much unlike young men, whom Aristotle thought unfit to hear moral philosophy.—*Troilus and Cressida*, ii, 1.

> Note.—Plato's most distinguished pupil, Aristotle, founder of the travelling school of philosophers, was one of the favourite ancient classics during the sixteenth century. From 1479 onwards, over twenty various editions of his writings sprang from English presses, up to 1637.

ARITHMETIC

Hamlet.—To divide him inventorially would dizzy the Arithmetic of memory, and it but yaw [deviate] neither, in respect of his quick sale.—*Hamlet*, v, 2.

ARTS. *See* LIBRARY.

AUTHORSHIP. *See* BALLAD, BOOK, LEARNING, LETTERS, LIBRARY, ODE, POESY, SONNET, WRITING.

BALLAD

Helena.—A divulged shame, traduced by odious Ballads.—*All's Well*, ii, 1.

Falstaff.—I will have it in a particular Ballad else, with mine own picture on top of it. —*2 King Henry IV*, iv, 3.

Armado.—Is there not a Ballad, boy, of the "King and the Beggar"?

Moth.—The world was very guilty of such a Ballad some three ages since, but I think now it is not to be found.—*Love's Labours*, i, 2.

Bottom.—I will get Peter Quince to write a Ballad of this dream.—*Midsummer Night's Dream*, iv, 1.

Clown.—What hast here? Ballads?

Mopsa.—Pray now, buy some! I love a Ballad in print . . . for then we are sure they are true.

Servant.—He utters them as if he had eaten Ballads.—*Winter's Tale*, iv, 4.

> Note.—In the absence of unborn newspapers in Shakespeare's days, almost every public event was chronicled in a doggerel ballad, or prose broadside.

BIBLE

First Clown.—How dost thou understand the Scripture? The Scripture says "Adam digged." Could he dig without arms?— *Hamlet*, v, 1.

King Henry.—Sins such as by God's Book are adjudged to death.—*2 King Henry VI*, ii, 3.

Gloster.—With old odd ends, stolen forth of Holy Writ.—*King Richard III*, i, 3.

Antonio.—The Devil can cite Scripture for his purpose.—*Merchant of Venice*, i, 3.

Iago.—

Trifles light as air, are to the jealous.

Confirmation strong as proofs of Holy Writ.
        —*Othello*, iii, 1.

> Note.—It seems singular that the Bible, as such, is never mentioned. It is referred to as "Holy Writ" or "Scripture," then common names for the Bible. America, as such, is named only once, though several times referred to by its then-usual name of "West Indies."

BINDING

Touchstone.—They that reap must sheaf and Bind.—*As You Like It*, iii, 2.

Dromio of Ephesus.—

If I last in this service
You must case me in Leather.
　　　　　—*Comedy of Errors, ii, 1.*

Posthumus.—A book! O, rare one! Be not, as is our fangled world, a garment nobler than that it covers.—*Cymbeline*, v, 4.

Shylock.—Fast bind; fast find. A proverb never stale in thrifty mind.—*Merchant of Venice, ii, 5.*

Lady Capulet.—

This precious "Book of Love"; this unbound lover,
To beautify him, only lacks a cover
That book in many eyes doth share the glory
That in gold-clasps locks in the golden story.
　　　　　—*Romeo and Juliet, i, 3.*

Juliet.—Was ever book containing such vile matter so fairly bound?—*Romeo and Juliet,* iii, 2.

Gremio.—Hark you, sir; I'll have them very fairly Bound.—*Taming of Shrew, i, 2.*

See also—FINISHER.

BLAZON. *See* PAINTING, PEDIGREE.

BODKIN

Hamlet.—When he himself might his quietus make with a bare Bodkin.—*Hamlet, iii, 1.*

Clown.—Betwixt the firmament and it you cannot thrust a Bodkin's point.—*Winter's Tale.—iii, 3.*

Note.—For untold generations a Bodkin has been in use by printers for adjusting type.

BOOK-MEN

Dull.—You two are Book-men! . . .—*Love's Labours, iv, 2.*

BOOK OF ARITHMETIC

Mercutio.—A rogue; a villain; that fights by the "Book of Arithmetic" . . .—*Romeo and Juliet,* iii, 1.

Note.—This may refer to the "Boke of Marchauntes" (Merchants) printed by T. Godfraye, 8vo, about 1534. Or, as is more likely, to the "Booke of good maners, 1507" mentioned by "Touchstone" in "As You Like It."

BOOK OF COMMON PRAYER

Duke of Buckingham.—

And see, a "Book of Prayer" in his hand
True ornament to know a holy man.
　　　　　—*King Richard III*, iii, 7.

Note.—If Shakespeare meant the "Book of Common Prayer" he has ante-dated it by nearly a century, as the first issue was in 1549.

BOOK OF MANNERS

Touchstone.—

O, sir, we quarrel, in print, by the book
As you have "Books for good manners."
　　　　　—*As You Like It,* v, 4.

Note.—This refers to Wynkyn De Worde's publication, "Booke of good maners, 1507," f'cap. 4to, of which copies are preserved at the British Museum and at Cambridge.

BOOK OF RIDDLES

Slender.—You have not the "Book of Riddles" about you, have you?—*Merry Wives, i, 1.*

Note.—The earliest recorded is the "Boke of a hundred riddles," folio, issued from the press of John Rastell, Barrister and Printer, about 1530. The sole known copy is at the Bodleian, Oxford. It was reprinted in octavo, pocket size, as the "Booke of merrie riddles, together with proper questions and witty proverbs, to make pleasant pastime..." 1617, black letter. The Bodleian owns versions of 1629 and 1631, but no pocket copies are now known earlier than 1617.

BOOK OF SECRETS

Soothsayer.—In nature's infinite "Book of Secrecy" a little I can read.—*Anthony and Cleopatra, i, 2.*

Note.—This appears to point to Albertus Magnus's "Boke of secretes," of which four editions were issued by William and Isaac Jaggard between 1595 and 1626.

BOOK OF SONGS AND SONNETS

Slender.—I had rather than forty shillings I had my "Book of songs and sonnets" here.
—*Merry Wives, i, 1.*

Note.—Slender's allusion is to Henry Howard, Earl of Surrey's "Songes and sonnettes," issued by R. Tottell in 1557, and reprinted in eight different surviving editions within the following thirty years. It may be added that George Turberville published through Henry Denham, in 1567, a small pocket volume of "Epitaphes, epigrams, songs and sonets!" Copies are to be seen at the Bodleian and at Cambridge.

BOOK OF SPORT

Hector.—

O, like a "Book of Sport" thou'lt read me o'er

But there's more in me than thou understandest.—*Troilus and Cressida*, iv, 5.

Note.—Our poet may have meant Dame Juliana Bernes, or Barnes's "Boke of hawking, hunting . . . 1486," first printed at St. Albans.

BOOKS

Brutus.—

Here's the Book I sought for so!

I put it in the pocket of my gown.

—*Julius Caesar*, iv, 3.

Earl of Worcester.—Say no more! and now I will unclasp a secret Book.—1 *King Henry IV*, i, 3.

Francis.—I'll be sworn upon all the Books in England.—1 *King Henry IV*, ii, 4.

Lady Percy.—He was the mark and glass, copy and Book, that fashioned others.—2 *King Henry IV*, ii, 3. •

Cade.—Here's a villain!

Smith.—Has a Book in his pocket with red letters in it.—2 *King Henry VI*, iv, 2.

Lord Say.—Because my Book preferred me to the King.—2 *King Henry VI*, iv, 2.

Duke of Buckingham.—A Beggar's Book outworths a Noble's blood.—*King Henry VIII*, i, 1.

Constable.—What hath it done, that it in golden letters should be set? Among the high tides in the Calendar.—*King John*, iii, 4.

Edgar.—Keep thy pen from lenders' Books, and defy the foul fiend.—*King Lear*, iii, 4.

Sir Nathaniel.—He hath never fed of the dainties that are bred in a Book.—*Love's Labours*, iv, 2.

Biron.—

And where that you have vowed to study, lords,

In that each of you have forsworn his Book

Can you still dream, and pore, and thereon look?

For when would you, my lord, or you, or you,

Have found the ground of study's excellence?

The Books, the Arts, the Academes,

That show, contain and nourish all the world.—*Love's Labours*, iv, 3.

Rosaline.—

Ware pencils! Ho! Let me not die your debtor.

My red Dominical! my golden letter!

—*Love's Labours*. v, 2.

Clerk (Nerissa).—We turned over many Books together; he is furnished with my opinion.—*Merchant of Venice*, iv, 1.

Shallow.—Keep a Gamester from his dice, and a good Student from his Book, and it is wonderful.—*Merry Wives*, iii, 1.

Lysander.—When I overlook love's stories, written in Love's richest Book.—*Midsummer Night's Dream*, ii, 3.

Othello.—This fair paper; this most goodly Book, made to write . . . upon.—*Othello*, vi, 2.

Duke.—The bloody Book of Law you shall yourself read in the bitter letter.—*Othello*, i, 3.

Pericles.—

Who has a Book of all that Monarchs do,

He's more secure to keep it shut, than shown.

—*Pericles*, i, 1.

Dionyza.—Her epitaphs in glittering golden characters, express a general praise to her.—*Pericles*, iv, 4.

Poet.—

O, that record could, with a backward look,

Even of five hundred courses of the sun,

Show me your image in some antique Book,

Since mind at first in character was done.

—*Sonnet* 59.

Bianca.—My Books and instruments shall be my company.—*Taming of Shrew*, i, 1.

Tranio.—And this small packet of Greek and Latin Books, if you accept them, then their worth is great.—*Taming of Shrew*, ii, 1.

Prospero.—Knowing I loved my Books . . . —*The Tempest*, i, 2.

Sir Toby.—Speaks three or four languages, word for word, without Book.—*Twelfth Night*, i, 3.

See also—BIBLE, BINDING, LIBRARY, PAINTING, PUBLISHING, READING, VOLUME, WRITING.

Note.—Lysander's reference appears to point to Boccaccio's "Decameron," first printed in English by Isaac Jaggard, 1620, to the manuscript of which Shakespeare doubtless had access years before.

The Duke's allusion in "Othello" probably meant the Statutes or Common Laws of the Realm.

Several other quotations obviously refer to the lovely illuminated monastic manuscripts of mediaeval days, with their pictorial and highly-burnished gilt initials. Rosaline's phrase "my red Dominical!" is explained by the fact that the mediaeval monks used the first seven letters of the alphabet, called "Dominical Letters," in their illuminated Calendars, to denote the Sundays of the year. They adopted the same seven letters to distinguish the position of notes on a stave of music.

BOOK-WORMS. *See* WORM-HOLES.

BRIGHT

Note.—Vautrollier printed Timothy Bright's "Treatise of Melancholy, 1586," which Shakespeare must have read, or corrected for press. It would make an attractive task for some capable student to compare Bright's book with our poet's mad characters, and thus discover what use he made of Bright. Also to find how far Bright served as a basis for Robert Burton's "Anatomy of Melancholy, 1621."

BROADSIDES

Pistol.—Fear we Broadsides? No! Let the fiend give fire.—*2 King Henry IV*, ii, 4.

Note.—As no newspapers existed until long after, the usual way to expose an abuse, attack a foe, or right a wrong, was to print a single sheet or "Broadside." These passed from hand to hand until worn out. They were often libellous, or rudely personal; hence the point of Pistol's remark.

BUYING

Boyet.—Did point you to buy them, along as you passed.—*Love's Labours*, ii, 1.

See also—SELLING.

CAESAR

Rosalind.—Caesar's thrasonical brag of "I came, saw and overcame."—*As You Like It*, v, 2.

Lord Say.—

Kent, in the "Commentaries" Caesar writ,
Is termed the civilest place of all this Isle.
　　　　　—*2 King Henry VI*, ii 7.

Note.—Between 1530 and 1640, ten editions of Caesar issued from English presses.

CALENDAR

Osrick.—To speak feelingly of him, he is the card or Calendar of gentry.—*Hamlet*, v, 2.

Brutus.—Look in the Calendar, and bring me word.—*Julius Caesar*, ii, 1.

King Richard.—Give me a Calendar.—*King Richard III*, v, 3.

Macbeth.—Let this pernicious hour stand, aye, accursed, in the Calendar.—*Macbeth*, iv, 1.

Fisherman.—If it be a day [that] fits you, search out of the Calendar, and nobody look after it.—*Pericles*, ii, 1.

Note.—Several of these references to Calendars are clearly author's chronological slips, as the plays are dated before European printing.

See also—ALMANAC.

CASE

Poet.—Accomplished in himself, not in his Case.—*Lover's Complaint*, line 116.

CHARACTERS

Orlando.—These trees shall be my Books and in their barks my thoughts I'll character.—*As You Like It*, iii, 2.

Imogen.—Learned indeed were that Astronomer that knew the stars as I his Characters. He'd lay the future open.—*Cymbeline*, iii, 2.

Lord Chief Justice.—Written down old, with all the Characters of age.—*2 King Henry IV*, i, 1.

Duke of Gloster.—I say, without Characters, fame lives long.—*King Richard III*, iii, 1.

Poet.—

Which on it had conceited Characters . . .
Thought, Characters, and Words, merely but
　　Art.—*Lover's Complaint*, lines 16 & 147.

Duke.—With Characters of brass, a forted [fortified] residence against the tooth of time, and razure of oblivion.—*Measure for Measure*, v, 1.

Isabel.—Even so may Angelo, in all his dressings, Characters, titles, forms, be an archvillain.—*Measure for Measure*, v, 1.

Anne Page.—Fairies use flowers for their Charactery.—*Merry Wives*, v, 5.

Cerimon.—A passport too! Apollo, perfect me in the Characters.—*Pericles*, ii, 2.

Poet.—
Since mind at first in Character was done . . .
While comments of your praise, richly compiled
Reserve their Character with golden quill . . .
What's in the brain that ink may Character?
—*Sonnets* 59, 85, 108.

Soldier.—

What's on this tomb I cannot read;
The Characters I'll take with wax;
Our Captain hath in every figure skill.
—*Timon of Athens*, v, 4.

Nestor.—

The purpose is perspicuous; even as substance
Whose grossness little Characters sum up.
—*Troilus and Cressida,* i, 3.

Troilus.—

Ay, Greek; and that shall be divulged well
In Characters as red as Mars . . .
—*Troilus and Cressida,* v, 2.

See also—ENGRAVING, LETTERS, PAINTED, TYPE.

CICERO

Cassius.—Did Cicero say anything?
Casca.—Ay; he spoke Greek.—*Julius Caesar,*
i, 2.
Messala.—Cicero is dead!—*Julius Caesar,* iv, 3.
Duke of Suffolk.—A Roman sworder and
banditto slave murdered sweet Tully.—*2
King Henry VI,* iv, 1.
Titus.—

Ah, boy; Cornelia never with more care
read to her sons,
Than she hath read to thee sweet poetry and
Tully's "Orator."
—*Titus Andronicus,* iv, 1.

Note.—Caxton first printed Cicero's "Boke of
Tulle of olde age" in 1481. Between that year and
1640, appeared no fewer than sixty various versions
of his writings, from English presses. Cicero thus
vied with Ovid for popularity in the sixteenth
century. Vautrollier published several editions of
Cicero, from 1575 onwards, all to be seen at the
British Museum.

CLAUDIAN

Thersites.—

And thou art as full of envy at his greatness,
As Cereberus is, at Proserpina's beauty.
—*Troilus and Cressida,* ii, 1.

Perdita.—O, Proserpina, for the flowers now
that, frighted, thou lettest fall.—*Winter's
Tale,* iv, 3.

Note.—No English edition of Claudian's "Rape
of Proserpine" appeared until 1617, the year after
our poet's death. Yet, like Helen of Troy's story, it
appears to have helped our bard when penning his
"Lucrece." Claudian himself is never mentioned by
Shakespeare.

COIGN

Menenius.—See you yond Coign of the Capi-
tol? yond corner-stone?—*Coriolanus,* v, 4.
Gower.—

By the four opposing Coigns
Which the world together joins.
—*Pericles,* iii, 1.

Note.—Here Shakespeare accurately pictures the
iron or steel frame, called a chase, holding, say, two
pages of type, making ready for press. Small and
hard wooden wedges, termed coigns or quoins, are
forced in, around the type, with a mallet, to make
the contents of the chase tight and safe. About 1700
a quaint and anonymous poetical Allegory appeared,
symbolizing the mystery of man's redemption. It
began—

"Great blest Master Printer, come
Into thy composing room . . ."

After spiritualizing the workman's sequence of
operations, he reaches the point of locking-up,
illustrating quoins—

"Let Quoins be thy sure election
Which admits of no rejection
With which our souls being joined about
Not the least grace can then fall out."

See also—LOCKING-UP.

COMMA

Hamlet.—
Peace should still her wheaten garland wear,
And stand a Comma between their amities.
—*Hamlet,* v, 2.
Poet.—No levelled malice infects one Comma
in the course.—*Timon of Athens,* i, 1.

Note.—This expression reminds us of the famous
omission, or commission, of a comma in a certain
State Act or Treaty which cost the nation concerned
about a million pounds to redeem.

COMPOSITION

King.—Frank nature, rather curious than in
haste, hath well Composed thee.—*All's
Well,* i, 2.

Antony.—If we Compose well here . . .—*Antony and Cleopatra,* ii, 2.

Bastard.—Mad World! mad Kings! mad Composition!—*King John,* ii, 1.

Angelo.—Her promised propositions came short of Composition.—*Measure for Measure,* v, 1.

Duke Theseus.—One that Composed your beauties . . .—*Midsummer Night's Dream,* i, 1.

Poet.—
Until life's Composition be re-cured
By those swift messengers returned from thee . . .
What the old world could say
To this Composed wonder of your frame.
—*Sonnets* 45 and 59.

Proteus.—
By wailful Sonnets, whose Composed rhymes
Should be full-fraught with serviceable vows.
—*Two Gentlemen,* iii, 2.

CONTENTS

Hymen.—If truth holds true Contents.—*As You Like It,* v, 4.

Iachimo.—Figures! Why, such and such, and the Contents of the story.—*Cymbeline,* ii, 2.

Poet.—And after reading what Contents it bears . . .—*Lover's Complaint,* line 19.

Poet.—To blot old Books and alter their Contents.—*Lucrece,* line 948.

Portia.—There are some shrewd Contents in yon same paper.—*Merchant of Venice,* iii, 2.

Stephano.—Kiss the Book! I will furnish it anon with new Contents.—*The Tempest,* ii, 2.

Note.—The "Lucrece" reference reminds us that one of the afflictions of early printers was the variation and corruption discovered in collating duplicate copies of old manuscripts. If the copying scribe thought of what seemed to him a good idea, he calmly embodied it in the text before him. Remembering this failing of scriveners our poet defines it as one of the effects of time.

See also—INDEX.

COPY

Poet.—
She carved thee for her seal, and meant thereby

Thou should'st Print more, nor let that Copy die . . .
Let him but Copy what in you is writ.
—*Sonnets* 11 and 84.

Viola.—If you will lead these graces to the grave, and leave the world no Copy.—*Twelfth Night,* i, 5.

CORRECTION

John of Gaunt.—
But since Correction lieth in those hands
Which made the fault, that we cannot Correct,
Put we our quarrel to the will of Heaven.
—*King Richard II,* i, 2.

Duke.—
Correction and instruction must both work,
Ere this rude beast will profit.
—*Measure for Measure,* iii, 2.

Poet.—
No bitterness that I will bitter think,
Nor double penance, to correct Correction.
—*Sonnet* 111.

CRAMP

Stephano.—O, touch me not; I am not Stephano, but a Cramp.—*The Tempest,* v, 1.

Note.—Shakspeare recalls here that Cramps are used in the bed of a printing machine to secure a tight hold on the Chase.

DEDICATION

Poet.—
The Dedicated words which writers use,
Of their fair subject . . .—*Sonnet* 82.

DEVIL

Rosalind.—'Tis not your inky brows . . .—*As You Like It,* iii, 5.

Falstaff.—And learning, a mere hoard of gold, kept by a Devil.—*2 King Henry IV,* iv, 3.

Macbeth.—The devil damn thee black, thou cream-faced loon.—*Macbeth,* v, 3.

Othello.—For here's a young and sweating Devil here, that commonly rebels. 'Tis a good Hand.—*Othello,* iii, 4.

Note.—The fitting connection of "Devil" and "Hand" is apparent to any printer. The apprentice, or youngest hand, of any printing staff is the "Jack-of-all-jobs," who fills odd time by picking up dropped type, cleansing utensils, conveying proofs, etc. Because he manages to convey daily much ink to his hands and face, he has been dubbed for centuries the printer's "devil." In the cradle days of the press he stood at the offside of the hand machine. So soon as the frisket was raised, he whisked the printed sheet off the tympan. If time dictated, he was despatched to the author's residence with urgent proofs. This reminds us of the anecdote about Dr. Samuel Johnson. When the printer (Andrew Millar) had from Johnson the final proof of Johnson's great folio Dictionary, Johnson asked the boy on return what Millar said. Upon learning that was the last proof of a job that had occupied so many years, said the boy, "Thank God!" "Oh," responded Johnson, "I am glad to hear that Andrew Millar thanks God for anything." As far back as 1683, Moxon's "Mechanick exercises" observed that "Devil" was an old trade nickname. From this we infer that it was common and familiar in our poet's day as now.

> "Old Lucifer, both kind and civil,
> To every Printer lends a 'Devil'
> But balancing accounts each winter,
> For every 'Devil' takes a Printer."

DOMINICAL. *See* BOOKS.

EDITION

Mrs. Page.—These are of the Second Edition.
—*Merry Wives*, ii, 1.

Note.—If Shakespeare assisted Field, or the brothers Jaggard in their Fleet Street bookshops, we may imagine him introducing popular books to buyers with some such remark.

ELEGIES. *See* POESY.

ENGRAVING

Talbot.—
Upon the which, that every one may read,
Shall be Engraved the sack of Orleans.
—1 *King Henry VI*, ii, 2.

Queen Elizabeth.—
Where should be Graven, if that right were right,
A pair of bleeding hearts, thereon Engrave
Edward and York.—*King Richard III*, iv, 4.

Poet.—
Then my digression is so vile, so base,
That it will live Engraven in my face.
—*Lucrece*, line 203.

Poet.—
That he shall never cut from memory
My sweet love's beauty, though my lover's life,
His beauty shall in these black lines be seen
And they shall live, and he in them still green.
—*Sonnet* 63.

Titus.—
I will go get a leaf of brass,
And with a gad of steel will write.
—*Titus Andronicus*, iv, 1.

Olivia.—
We will draw the curtain and show you the
picture . . .
'Tis Engra'en sir; It will endure wind and
weather.—*Twelfth Night*, i, 5.

Julia.—
Who art the table, wherein all my thoughts
Are visibly charactered and Engraved.
—*Two Gentlemen*, ii, 7.

EPITOME

Volumnia.—This is a poor Epitome of yours, which, by the interpretation of full time, may show like all yourself.—*Coriolanus*, v, 3.

ERRORS

Antipholus of Syracuse.—Smothered in Errors, feeble, shallow, weak.—*Comedy of Errors*, iii, 2.

Messala.—
A hateful Error, melancholy's child,
Why dost thou show, to the apt thoughts of
men,
The things that are not . . .
—*Julius Caesar*, v, 3.

Armado.—Pardon, sir; Error; he is not quantity enough for that worthy's thumb.—*Love's Labours*, v, 1.

Poet.—
If this be Error, and upon me proved,
I never writ; nor no man ever loved. . . .
Book both my wilfulness and Errors down
And on just proof surmise accumulate.
—*Sonnets* 116 and 117.

Cressida.—
The Error of our eye directs our mind
What Error leads must err! O, then
conclude,
Minds swayed by eyes are full of turpitude.
—*Troilus and Cressida*, v, 2.

Proteus.—That one Error fills him with faults.—*Two Gentlemen*, v, 4.

EXCLAMATION

Dogberry.—For I hear as good Exclamation on your worship as of any man in the city.—*Much Ado*, iii, 5.

FIGURES

Brutus.—
> Thou hast no Figures, nor no fantasies,
> Which busy care draws in the brains of men.
> > —*Julius Caesar*, ii, 1

Earl of Worcester.—
> He apprehends a world of Figures here
> But not the form of what he should attend.
> > —1 *King Henry IV*, i, 3.

Lord Bardolph.—
> We fortify in paper and in Figures,
> Using the names of men, instead of men.
> > —2 *King Henry IV*, i, 3.

Fool.—Now thou art an "O" without a Figure.
—*King Lear*, i, 4.

Armado.—A most fine Figure.

Moth.—To prove you a cypher.—*Love's Labours*, i, 2.

Ford.—She works by charms, by spells, by the Figure, and such daubery.—*Merry Wives*, iv, 2.

Poet.—Figures of delight, drawn after you; you pattern of all those.—*Sonnet* 98.

Speed.—Why, she woos you by a Figure.
Valentine.—What Figure?
Speed.—By a letter. I should say.—*Two Gentlemen*, ii, 1.

FINISHER

Helena.—
> He that of greatest works is Finisher,
> Oft does them by the weakest minister.
> > —*All's Well*, ii, 1.

FOLDING

Antipholus of Syracuse.—The Folded meaning of your words' deceit.—*Comedy of Errors*, iii, 2.

Hamlet.—Folded the writ up in form of the other; subscribed it; gave it the impression.
—*Hamlet*, v, 2.

King John.—They shoot but calm words, Folded up in smoke.—*King John*, ii, 1.

Poet.—Of Folded Schedules had she many a one which she perused.—*Lover's Complaint*, line 43.

FOLIO

Armado.—I am for whole volumes in Folio.—*Love's Labours*, i, 2.

FORMES

Holofernes.—Full of Forms, figures, shapes, objects.—*Love's Labours*, iv, 2.

FULLPOINTS. *See* POINTS.

GALEN

Falstaff.—I have read the cause of his effects in "Galen" . . .—2 *King Henry IV*, i, 2.

Host.—What says my Æsculapius?—my Galen? . . .—*Merry Wives*, ii, 3.

> *Note.*—Galen, or Claudius Galenus, a famous Greek physician, was born at Pergamus in Illyria, where, after studying in various cities, he settled in A.D. 158. His extensive medical writings were accepted as authoritative for centuries after his death. Between 1521 and 1586 there were seven English printings of his works.

GUICCIARDINI

> *Note.*—Vautrollier printed an English translation of Ludovic Guicciardini's "Description of the low countries . . . 1567." In this book occurs one of the earliest accounts of European invention of printing, at Haarlem, which is thus described in the "Batavia" of Andrian Junius, 1575: "This person (Coster) during his afternoon walk, in the vicinity of Haarlem, amused himself with cutting letters out of the bark of beech trees, and with these, the characters being inverted, as in seals, he printed small sentences." The idea is adopted by Shakespeare in "As You Like It." *See* Orlando's phrase (under CHARACTERS). Our poet also uses the surname of Coster, slightly altered, as Costard, in "Love's Labours" cast.

HERALDRY

Poet.—
> This Heraldry in Lucrece' face was seen.
> Argued by beauty's red and virtue's white.
> > —*Lucrece*, line 64.

Othello.—
> A liberal hand! The hearts of old gave hands.
> But our new Heraldry is—hands, not hearts.—*Othello*, iii, 4.

Petrucio.—A Herald, Kate? O, put me in thy books.—*Taming of Shrew*, ii, 1.

> *Note.*—Othello's allusion may be meant as a humorous sally upon William Jaggard's then newly-acquired crest, which displayed a Hand, dexter, grasping the Mace of Authority.

HIPPOCRATES

Sir Hugh Evans.—He has no more knowledge in Hibocrates and Galen . . . withal . . .
—*Merry Wives*, iii, 1.

Note.—The "Father of Medicine," Hippocrates, born at Cos, in 460 B.C., was a contemporary of Socrates and Plato. His "Prognosticacion," printed by R. Wyer, appeared about 1530. A Latin edition of his "Aphorisms" came from the press of Wm. Seres in 1567. Both books are at the British Museum.

HOLINSHED

Volumnia.—Whose Chronicle thus writ: The man was noble; but with his last attempt, he wiped it out.—*Coriolanus, v, 3.*

Hamlet.—They are the Abstracts and brief Chronicles of the time.—*Hamlet, ii, 2.*

Fluellen.—As I have read in the "Chronicles" . . .—*King Henry V, iv, 7.*

Queen Katherine.—

After my death, I wish no other herald,
No other speaker of my living actions . . .
But such an honest Chronicler. . .
     —*King Henry VIII, iv, 2.*

Christopher Sly.—The Slys are no rogues! Look in the "Chronicles" . . .—*Taming of Shrew,* Induction.

Hector.—Good old "Chronicle," that hast so long walked hand in hand with time.—*Troilus and Cressida, iv. 5.*

Note.—Our poet's great debt to Raphael Holinshed, from whom he drew freely for his "Chronicle" plays, is often pointed out. If he corrected the proofs of the three folio volumes in 1585-86, as is extremely probable, then familiarity with the contents is easily explained.

HOMER

Note.—Though not pointedly named, Homer's vivid verse is instantly recalled by the cast and incidents of the entire play of "Troilus and Cressida." Between 1580 and 1634 there were fourteen English-printed versions of Homer.

HORACE

Holofernes.—Or rather, as Horace says . . . —*Love's Labours, iv, 2.*

Chiron.—

O, 'tis a verse in Horace; I know it well.
I read it in the Grammar long ago.
     —*Titus Andronicus, iv, 2.*

Note.—Numerous editions of Horace appeared in Latin or English, from 1566 onwards. His "Odes" and "Satires" formed ordinary grammar-school text-books of the period.

HUNDRED MERRY TALES

Beatrice.—That I had my good wit out of the "Hundred merry tales" . . .—*Much Ado, ii, 1.*

Note.—The first issue recorded of this early Jest Book is the folio printed by John Rastell, about 1525, of which the sole surviving perfect copy is at the British Museum. Fragments of eight leaves of a second copy are preserved at Shakespeare's birthplace. It was reprinted in 1526, and again about 1535.

ILLUMINATION. *See* PAINTING.

IMPOSING

Diana.—Let death and honesty go with your Impositions.—*All's Well, iv, 4.*

Osrick.—He has Imponed, as I take it, six French rapiers and poinards . . .

Hamlet.—Why this "Imponed" as you call it? —*Hamlet, v, 2.*

Troilus.—Thinking it harder for our Mistress to devise Imposition, than for us to undergo any difficulty imposed.—*Troilus and Cressida, iii, 2.*

IMPRESSION

Coriolanus.—

. . . Sink, my knee, in the earth;
Of thy deep duty, more Impression show.
     —*Coriolanus, v, 3.*

Boyet.—His heart . . . with your print Impressed.—*Love's Labours, ii, 1.*

Malvolio.—And the Impressure, her "Lucrece," which she uses to seal.—*Twelfth Night, ii, 5.*

Duke.—This weak Impress of love is as a figure.—*Two Gentlemen, iii, 2.*

IMPRINTING. *See* PRINTING.

INDENT

Oliver.—And, with Indented glides, did slip away into a bush.—*As You Like It, iv, 3.*

King Henry.—Shall we buy treason, and Indent with fears?—1 *King Henry IV, i, 3.*

Hotspur.—It shall not wind with such a deep Indent.—1 *King Henry IV, iii, 1.*

INDEX

Queen.—That roars so loud, and thunders, in the Index.—*Hamlet, iii, 4.*

Duke of Buckingham.—As Index to the story we late talked of.—*King Richard III,* ii, 2.

Queen Margaret.—Flattering Index of a direful pageant.—*King Richard III,* iv, 4.

Iago.—Index and obscure prologue to the history . . .—*Othello,* ii, 1.

Nestor.—And in such Indexes . . . there is seen the baby figure of the giant mass of things to come at large.—*Troilus and Cressida,* i, 3.

See also—CONTENTS.

INK

Pisanio.—O, damned paper! black as the Ink that is on thee.—*Cymbeline,* iii, 2.

Sir Nathaniel.—He hath not drunk Ink. His intellect is not replenished. — *Love's Labours,* iv, 2.

Princess.—Beauteous as Ink! A good conclusion.—*Love's Labours,* v, 2.

Dogberry.—Moreover, sir; which indeed is not under white and black.—*Much Ado,* v, 1.

Poet.—That in black Ink my love may still shine bright.—*Sonnet 66.*

Sir Toby.—Taunt him with the license of Ink! Let there be gall enough in thy Ink, though thou write with a goose pen.—*Twelfth Night,* iii, 2.

LEAD

King Lear.—Mine own tears do scald like molten Lead.—*King Lear,* iv, 7.

Moth.—As swift as Lead, sir.—*Love's Labours,* iii, 1.

Servant.—I had as lief bear so much Lead.—*Merry Wives,* iv, 2.

Poet.—

Mine eyes are turned to fire; my heart to Lead:

Heavy heart's Lead, melt mine eyes' red fire.

  —*Venus and Adonis,* line 107.

See also—METAL.

LEARNING

Sir Nathaniel.—Truly, the epithets are sweetly varied, like a scholar at the least.—*Love's Labours,* iv, 2.

Lucentio.—A course of Learning and ingenious studies.—*Taming of Shrew,* i, 1.

Gremio.—O, this Learning! What a thing it is.

  —*Taming of Shrew,* i, 2.

LEAVES

Marcus.—See, brother, see! Note how she quotes the Leaves.—*Titus Andronicus,* iv, 1.

LETTERS

Earl of Westmorland.—

Whose learning and good Letters peace hath tutored,

Whose white investments figure innocence.

  —2 *King Henry IV,* iv, 1.

Holofernes.—I will look again on the intellect of the Letter.—*Love's Labours,* iv, 2.

Rosaline.—Much in the Letters, nothing in the praise.—*Love's Labours,* v, 2.

See also—BOOK, CHARACTERS, ENGRAVING.

LIBRARY

Lucentio.—Nursery of Arts. — *Taming of Shrew,* i, 1.

Prospero.—

Me, poor man! My Library was dukedom large enough.

Knowing I loved my books, he furnished me, from my own Library,

With volumes that I prize above my dukedom.—*The Tempest,* i, 2.

Titus.—

Some book there is that she desires to see . . .

But thou art deeper read, and better skilled

Come and take choice of all my Library,

And so beguile thy sorrow . . .

  —*Titus Andronicus,* iv, 1.

See also—BIBLE, BINDING, BOOKS, LEARNING, READING, VOLUME.

LOCKING-UP

Cornelius.—

No danger in what show of death it makes,

More than the Locking-up the spirits a time.

  —*Cymbeline,* i, 6.

King Henry.—

And he but Naked, though Locked-up in steel,

Whose conscience with injustice is corrupted.

  —2 *King Henry VI,* iii, 2.

Claudio.—As fast Locked-up in sleep as guiltless labour.—*Measure for Measure,* iv, 2.

Nestor.—But this, thy countenance, still Locked in steel, I never saw till now.—*Troilus and Cressida,* iv, 5.

Florizel.—Gifts she looks from me are packed and Locked-up in my heart.—*Winter's Tale,* iv, 4.

See also—COIGN.

> *Note.*—When the locked "forme" was worked off, and unlocked on a table, the chase would be removed, leaving the pages of type all unprotected or "naked." King Henry's reference is a keen remembrance of a printing workshop.

LUCAN

Duke,—Marcus Luccicos! Is not he in town? —*Othello,* i, 3.

Candidus.—At Pharsalia, where Caesar fought with Pompey.—*Antony and Cleopatra,* iii, 7.

> *Note.*—Lucan (or Marcus Lucanus) is not quoted by our poet, though his name appears to have been adapted in the above phrase. From 1589 to 1635 there were ten various English-printed editions of his "Pharsalia."

LUCIAN

Hamlet.—This is one Lucianus, nephew to the King.—*Hamlet,* iii, 2.

> *Note.*—Shakespeare uses his name for this character, and perhaps was familiar with the "Dialogues" of Lucian (or Lucianus) of which six different editions came from English presses between 1521 and 1634.

MADRIGAL

Sir Hugh Evans.—Melodious birds sing Madrigals.—*Merry Wives,* iii, 1.

See also—PRICK SONG.

> *Note.*—The madrigal excerpts, sung at this point by Evans, are taken from Marlowe's part song, "Come, live with me, and be my love," first printed in the little anthology, by our poet (and others) entitled the "Passionate Pilgrim . . . issued by Wm. Jaggard, 1599, 1604, and 1612."

MANTUAN

Holofernes.—

> . . . Ah, good old Mantuan!
> I may speak of thee as the traveller does of Venice,
> Old Mantuan! Old Mantuan!
> Who understandeth thee not, loves thee not.
>   —*Love's Labours,* iv, 2.

> *Note.*—Mantuan, whose real name was Baptista Spagnuoli, was a favourite grammar-school author in the sixteenth century. His "Bucolics" first

appeared in 1523, and passed through twelve editions, in England, up to 1638. His "Eclogues" came out in 1567 and again in 1572, and were used as Latin exercises by beginners, as an alternative to Virgil.

MARGENT

Horatio.—I knew you must be edified by the Margent, ere you had done.—*Hamlet,* v, 2.

Princess.—

> As would be crammed up in a sheet of paper,
> Writ on both sides the leaf, Margin and all.
>   —*Love's Labours,* v, 2.

Poet.—

> Nor read the subtle-shining secrecies,
> Writ in the glassy Margents of such books.
>   —*Lucrece,* line 102.

> *Note.*—In Tudor days "Margent" was the rule rather than the exception. Our word "Margin" appears to be a corruption.

MAR-TEXT

Touchstone.—A most vile Mar-text.—*As You Like It,* v, 1.

METAL

Angelo.—As dear as all the Metal in your shop will answer.—*Comedy of Errors,* iv, 1.

Duchess of Gloster.—That Metal, that self-mould that fashioned thee, made him a man. —*King Richard II,* i, 2.

Armado.—Is not lead a Metal, heavy, dull, and slow?—*Love's Labours,* iii, 1.

Angelo.—

> Let there be some more test made of my Metal,
> Before so noble and so great a figure be stamped upon it.
>   —*Measure for Measure,* i, 1.

See also—LEAD.

MOULDING

Sicilius.—Great nature, like his ancestry, moulded the stuff so fair.—*Cymbeline,* v, 4.

Wolsey.—Now I feel of what coarse Metal ye are Moulded.—*King Henry VIII,* iii, 2.

Poet.—For stealing Moulds from heaven that were divine.—*Venus and Adonis,* line 730.

MUSIC. *See* BALLAD, BOOK OF SONGS, CANZONET, MADRIGAL, PRICK-SONG, RHYMES.

NEWS

Speed.—What News, then, in your paper?

Launce.—The blackest News that ever thou heardest.

Speed.—Why, man, how black?

Launce.—Why, as black as ink.—*Two Gentlemen*, iii, 1.

NONPAREIL

Enobarbus.—Spake you of Caesar? How! The Nonpareil!—*Antony and Cleopatra*, iii, 2.

Posthumus.—

My mother seemed the Diana of that time,
As doth my wife the Nonpareil of this.
　　　　　　　　　　—*Cymbeline*, ii, 5.

Macbeth.—If thou didst it, thou art the Nonpareil.—*Macbeth*, iii, 4.

Viola.—Though you were crowned the Nonpareil of Beauty.—*Twelfth Night*, i, 5.

Caliban.—The beauty of his daughter; he himself calls her a Nonpareil.—*The Tempest*, iii, 2.

Note.—In the sixteenth century, varieties in typesizes were few indeed, compared with modern resources. Sizes familiar to Shakespeare would be "Canon, Great Primer, Pica, Long Primer, Brevier," and a smaller fount called "Nonpareil," newly introduced from Holland, admired for its beauty and handiness. The name became a synonym for anything remarkable.

NUMBERING

Rosaline.—

Nay, I have verses too, I thank Biron.
The numbers true, and were the Numbering too . . .—*Love's Labours*, v, 2.

ODE

Dumaine.—Once more I'll read the Ode that I have writ.—*Love's Labours*, iv, 3.

See also—POESY.

OVER-COUNT

Antony.—Thou knowest how much we do Over-Count.—*Antony and Cleopatra*, ii, 6.

OVER-READ

Decius.—Over-read, at your best leisure.—*Julius Caesar*, ii, 1.

King Henry.—Bid them Over-read these letters . . .—2 *King Henry IV*, iii, 1.

Edmund.—It is a letter from my brother, that I have not all Over-read.—*King Lear*, i, 2.

Duke.—You shall, anon, Over-read it, at your pleasure.—*Measure for Measure*, iv, 2.

OVER-SET

Lord Bardolph.—And, since we are Over-Set, venture again.—2 *King Henry IV*, i, 1.

OVID

Touchstone.—I am here with thee and thy goats, as the most capricious Poet, honest Ovid, was, among the Goths.—*As You Like It*, iii, 3.

Holofernes.—Ovidius Naso was the man; and why, indeed, "Naso," but for smelling out the odoriferous flowers of fancy.—*Love's Labours*, iv, 2.

Tranio.—As Ovid, be an outcast quite abjured.—*Taming of Shrew*, i, 1.

Lucentio.—Profit you in what you read?

Bianca.—What, Master, read you? First resolve me that!

Lucentio.—I read that I profess; the "Art to love" (by Ovid).—*Taming of Shrew*, iv, 2.

Titus.—What book is that she tosseth so?

Lucius.—Grandsire, 'tis Ovid's "Metamorphosis" . . .—*Titus Andronicus*, iv, 1.

Note.—Vautrollier published Ovid's "Metamorphosis," his "Epistles," and his "Art of Love." While Shakespeare rarely mentions a Latin poet, still more seldom a Greek one, yet he quotes Ovid several times. This is natural, for Ovid and Cicero were the most popular ancient classics in his day. Over sixty different English printings are recorded of each author, either in Latin or English, between 1513 and 1640.

PAGE

Poet.—But makes antiquity for aye his Page.—*Sonnet* 108.

Note.—The epitaph over Shakespeare's tomb ends up: "Leaves living art but Page to serve his wit."

PAINTING

Biron.—

Lend me the flourish of all gentle tongues,
Fie! Painted rhetoric . . .
　　　　　　　　　　—*Love's Labours*, iv, 3.

Host.—'Tis Painted about with the "Story of the Prodigal," fresh and new.—*Merry Wives*, iv, 5.

Benedict.—Let me be vilely Painted, and in such great letters.—*Much Ado*, i, 1.

Cassio.—One that excels the quirks of Blazoning pens.—*Othello*, ii, 1.

Olivia.—
Thy tongue, thy face, thy limbs, action, and spirit,
Do give thee five-fold Blazon . . .
　　　　　　—*Twelfth Night*, i, 5.

Note.—In our poet's days, a "Painted Book" meant an illuminated volume. To "Blazon" a pedigree signified, to colour and gild the coats-of-arms.

PAMPHLET

Bishop of Winchester.—
Comest thou with deep premeditated lines?
With written Pamphlet studiously devised?

Note.—With a playful question of this kind, we may imagine Shakespeare greeting an acquaintance; some author just arrived in bookshop, or printery, with a parcel of MS.

PAPER

Cinna.—Well, I will hie, and so bestow these Papers, as you bade me.—*Julius Caesar*, i, 3.

Peto.—Nothing but Papers, my lord!—1 *King Henry IV*, ii, 4.

Doll Tear-sheet.—Thou Paper-faced villain.— 2 *King Henry IV*, v, 4.

Duchess of Gloster.—Mailed up in shame, with Papers on my back.—2 *King Henry VI*, ii, 4.

Earl of Gloster.—What Paper were you reading?—*King Lear*, i, 2.

Edmund.—If the matter of this Paper be certain, you have mighty business in hand.— *King Lear*, iii, 5.

Duke of Albany.—Read thine own evil: No tearing: Knowest thou this Paper?—*King Lear*, v, 3.

King Richard.—
Make dust our Paper, and with rainy eyes,
Write sorrow on the bosom of the earth.
　　　　　　—*King Richard II*, iii, 2.

Sir Nathaniel.—He hath not ate Paper, as it were: he hath not drunk ink.—*Love's Labours*, iv, 2.

Biron.—Here comes one with a Paper.

King.—I'll drop the Paper, sweet leaves . . . —*Love's Labours*, iv, 3.

Clown.—He's in for a commodity of brown Paper.—*Measure for Measure*, iv, 3.

Benedict.—Shall quips and sentences, and these Paper bullets of the brain, awe a man?— *Much Ado*, ii, 3.

Lodovico.—He did not call: he is busy in the Paper.—*Othello*, iv, 1.

Lodovico.—Now here is another discontented Paper, found in his pocket.—*Othello*, v, 2.

Apemantus.—I fear me, thou wilt give away thyself in Paper shortly.—*Timon of Athens*, i, 2.

PAPER MILL

Jack Cade.—Contrary to the King, his crown and dignity, thou hast built a Paper-Mill . . —2 *King Henry VI*, iv, 7.

PARACELSUS

Parolles.—So I say, both of Galen and Paracelsus.—*All's Well*, ii, 3.

Note.—Paracelsus, a Swiss physician, alchemist, and mystic, was a queer "mixture," like his writings. His real name was Theophrastus Bombastus, born 1493, died 1541. As a violent revolutionary in medical art, his theories provoked so much enmity, he was forced into a wandering and unsettled life. But his wide knowledge and practice led, in no small measure, to a more general scientific study of nature, to the ultimate benefit of humanity.

PARCHMENT

Dromio of Ephesus.—
If the skin were Parchment, and the blows you gave were ink,
Your own handwriting would tell you what I think.—*Comedy of Errors*, iii, 1.

Hamlet.—Is not Parchment made of sheep-skins?

Horatio.—Ay, my lord, and of calf-skins too. —*Hamlet*, v, 1.

Antony.—Here's a Parchment with the seal of Caesar.—*Julius Caesar*, iii, 2.

Jack Cade.—Is not this a lamentable thing? That of the skin of an innocent lamb should be made Parchment: That Parchment, being scribbled over, should undo a man.— 2 *King Henry VI*, iv, 2.

King John.—I am a scribbled form, drawn with a pen, upon a Parchment.—*King John,* v, 7.

John of Gaunt.—Bound in with shame, with inky blots, and rotten Parchment bonds.—*King Richard II,* ii, 1.

Camillo.—Nor brass, nor stone, nor Parchment . . .—*Winter's Tale,* i, 2.

> *Note.*—In Elizabethan days, Parchment and Vellum were synonymous terms. Now they mean totally different substances, though it is a common error to hear one mis-called by the name of the other. Vellum is an animal skin; while Parchment is a vellum imitation, of paper origin.

PEDIGREE

Duke of Exeter.—Willing you overlook this Pedigree.—*King Henry V,* ii, 4.

Earl of Warwick.—

Can Oxford, that did ever fence the right,
Now buckler falsehood with a Pedigree?
  —*3 King Henry VI,* iii, 3.

See also—PAINTING.

PEN. *See* WRITING.

PERIOD

Guard.—The star is fallen, and time is at his Period.—*Antony and Cleopatra,* iv, 12.

King Henry.—There's his Period; to sheathe his knife in us.—*King Henry VIII,* i, 2.

Queen Margaret.—O, let me make the Period to my curse.—*King Richard III,* i, 3.

Poet.—

Which to her oratory adds more grace,
She puts the Period often from his place.
  —*Lucrece,* line 565.

Falstaff.—I have lived long enough: This is the Period of my ambition.—*Merry Wives,* iii, 3.

Mrs. Ford.—There would be no Period to the jest, should he not be publicly shamed.—*Merry Wives,* iv, 2.

Theseus.—Make Periods in the midst of sentences . . .—*Midsummer Night's Dream,* v, 1.

Silvia.—A pretty Period! . . .—*Two Gentlemen,* ii, 1.

See also—POINTS.

PICTURE

Iachimo.—I will write all down; such and such Pictures.—*Cymbeline,* ii, 2.

Rosaline.—O, he hath drawn my Picture in his letter.—*Love's Labours,* v, 2.

Poet.—

Many there were that did his Picture get,
To serve their eyes, and in it put their mind.
  —*Lover's Complaint,* line 134.

Poet.—

This Picture she advisedly perused,
And chid the Painter for his wondrous skill.
  —*Lucrece,* line 1527.

Poet.—

To find where your true image Pictured lies
Which in my bosom's shop is hanging still.
  —*Sonnet* 24.

PLAUTUS

Polonius.—Seneca cannot be too heavy: nor Plautus too light.—*Hamlet,* ii, 2.

> *Note.*—To the "Menaecmi," of Plautus, our poet had occasion to be grateful, for it furnished him with the plot of the "Comedy of Errors." The first English edition of this "pleasant comedie" of Plautus emerged in 1595.

POESY

Rosalind.—

Hangs Odes upon hawthorns, and Elegies on brambles . . .

Are you he that hangs the Verses on the trees?—*As You Like It,* iii, 2.

Holofernes.—

But for the elegancy, facility, and golden cadence of Poesy . . .

I will prove these verses to be very unlearned; neither savouring of Poetry, wit, or invention.—*Love's Labours,* iv, 2.

Poet.—

Every alien hath got my use . . .
And under these their Poesy disperse.
  —*Sonnet* 78.

Tranio.—

Balk logic with acquaintance that you have,
And practise rhetoric in your common talk,
Music and Poesy use to quicken you
The mathematics and the metaphysics . . .
  —*Taming of Shrew,* i, 1.

Baptista.—
> And, for I know, she taketh most delight
> In music, instruments, and Poetry.
> > —*Taming of Shrew,* i, 1.

Gremio.—
> Well read in Poetry, and other books;
> Good ones, I warrant ye . . .
> > —*Taming of Shrew,* i, 2.

Poet.—Our Poesy is as a gum, which oozes from whence . . . nourished.—*Timon of Athens,* i, 1.

Duke of Milan.—Much is the force of heaven-bred Poesy.—*Two Gentlemen,* iii, 2.

POET

Biron.—
> Never durst Poet touch a pen to write,
> Until his inks were tempered with love's sighs.—*Love's Labours,* iv, 3.

Poet.—
> Since he died, and Poets better prove,
> Theirs' for their style I'll read: his for his love.—*Sonnet 32.*

POINTS

Pistol.—Come we to Full Points here, and are Etceteras nothing?—2 *King Henry IV,* ii, 4.

Gloster.—Why, brother, wherefore stand you on nice Points?—3 *King Henry VI,* iv, 7.

Earl of Kent.—My Point and Period will be thoroughly wrought . . .—*King Lear,* iv, 7.

Bottom.—Read the names of the Actors, and so grow to a Point.—*Midsummer Night's Dream,* i, 2.

Pericles.—And make my senses credit thy relation to Points that seem impossible.—*Pericles,* v, 1.

See also—PERIOD.

> *Note.*—So rarely do we find the term "Full Points" used for Full Stops, outside printing circles, that this is a very significant bit of evidence.

PORTRAIT. *See* PICTURE.

PREFACE

Suffolk.—
> Tush, my good lord, this superficial tale
> Is but a Preface of her worthy praise.
> > —1 *King Henry VI,* v, 5.

PRESS

Hamlet.—All saws of books, all forms, all Pressures past . . .—*Hamlet,* i, 5.

Mrs. Ford.—He cares not what he would put into the Press, when he would put us two . . .—*Merry Wives,* ii, 1.

> *Note.*—This "Press" allusion serves to remind us that in Shakespeare's days special "'Patents" or sole rights were granted to certain printers, which secured to them the profitable monopoly of given publications. Severe pains and penalties awaited those caught trespassing on these legal rights. Offenders could be fined, or imprisoned by the Stationers' Guild, without resort to any legal court. Presses, plant, stock-in-trade, in part or entirety, could be confiscated or destroyed by order of the Stationers' Court. Despite the risk, several printers constantly practised piracy. It was perhaps this disregard of consequences that led to Mrs. Ford's remark. Among the monopolists were the Stationers' Company itself. They issued all Almanacs. The King's Printers printed all Bibles, and Government issues. John Jaggard published all the law books; Wm. and Issac Jaggard all the city official documents, and Playhouse playbills; Reynold Wolfe specialized in all works set in Hebrew, Greek or Latin; the East, or Este, family cornered music printing; Seres held the right for Primers, Psalters, and Prayer-books; Henry Denham reserved the New Testament in Welsh; another prepared all the apprentice indenture forms; one, for issuing broad.sides; another, school-books; and so on. In these "tied" specialities, it was usual to print a Caveat. Commonly the warning took the Latin form of "Cum privilegio ad imprimendum solum." This phrase stands, for instance, in Vautrollier's monopoly of Beza's "New Testament" and Shakespeare adopts it, with witty aptness, thus :—

> Lucentio.—"And what of all this?"

> Biondello.—"I cannot tell, except they are busied about a counterfeit assurance. Take you assurance of her, 'Cum privilegio ad imprimendum solum.' To the church, take the Priest, Clerk, and some sufficient honest witnesses."—*Taming of Shrew,* iv, 4.

> *Note.*—Herein is another word peculiar to the book trade. The term "Counterfeit" then meant "duplicate" or "reprint." The "tied" monopolies described, instead of being benefits to all concerned, grew into abuses, oppressive and restrictive. Books of lasting merit perished forgotten, for want of enterprise in the Patentee. Folly, in the Star Chamber, kept a brake on intelligence and progress. As Shakespeare says :—
> > "Art, made tongue-tied by authority,
> > And Folly, Doctor-like, controlling skill."
> > > —*Sonnet 66.*

PRICK-SONG

Duke.—

Give me some music! . . . that piece of song,

That old and antique song we heard last night.—*Twelfth Night*, ii, 4.

King Henry.—Lulled with sounds of sweetest melody.—2 *King Henry IV*, iii, 1.

Helena.—My tongue shall catch your tongue's sweet melody.—*Midsummer Night's Dream*, i, 1.

Fairies.—Philomel, with melody, sing in our sweet lullaby.—*Midsummer Night's Dream*, ii, 3.

Simonides.—

For your sweet music, this last night, I do protest,

My ears were never better fed with

Such delightful pleasing harmony.

Sir, you are music's master.—*Pericles*, ii, 5.

Mercutio.—

He fights as you sing Prick-Song;

One, two and the third in your bosom.

　　　　　—*Romeo and Juliet*, ii, 4.

Lucentio.—Give me leave to read philosophy, and, while I pause, serve in your harmony.

—*Taming of Shrew*, iii, 1.

Sir Andrew.—A mellifluous voice; as I am true knight.—*Twelfth Night*, ii, 3.

See also—CANZONET, MADRIGAL.

Note.—A "Prick-Song" is a theme or poem, set in harmonized parts, for several voices, such as a Canzonet, Madrigal, or Part-song.

PRINTING

Cymbeline.—Some more time must wear the Print of his remembrance out.—*Cymbeline*, ii, 3.

Chorus.—

Think, when we talk of horses, that you see them,

Printing their proud hoofs in the receiving earth.—*King Henry V*, Chorus.

Note.—Deep indentation on the receiving paper, by the arm of a strong machinist, pulling the bar with too great vigour, is suggested by this quotation.

Queen Margaret.—Oh, could this kiss be Printed in thy hand.—2 *King Henry VI*, iii, 2.

Jack Cade.—Thou hast most traitorously corrupted the youth of the realm, in erecting a Grammar School, and whereas before, our forefathers had no other books but the score and tally, thou hast caused Printing to be used.—2 *King Henry VI*, iv, 7.

Note.—In the early story of "Doctor Faustus," the Devil, in a moment of strange aberration, is said to have assisted him in rapid multiplication of the first printed Bibles. This popular story was widely known, and created among the ignorant a prejudice against the original printing presses. It was to this dark bigotry that Jack Cade appealed. At this point, perhaps, it is well to observe that all our chroniclers date the cradle of English printing some years too early. Shakespeare copies the error by putting back the date to 1450, the time of Jack Cade's insurrrection. While the precise date is still as uncertain as in Queen Elizabeth's reign, we now know it was in or about 1475.

Boyet.—His heart, like an agate, with your Print impressed.—*Love's Labours*, ii, 1.

Costard.—I will do it, sir, in Print.—*Love's Labours*, iii, 1.

Note.—Would Costard, a country bumpkin, never nominally within a hundred miles of a press, use this expression, unless the author's mind was teeming with such?

Mrs. Page.—He will Print them, out of doubt. —*Merry Wives*, ii, 1.

Duke Theseus.—

To whom you are but as a form in wax, by him Imprinted,

And within his power, to leave the figure, or disfigure it.

　　　　　—*Midsummer Night's Dream*, i, 1.

Leonato.—The story that is Printed in her blood.—*Much Ado*, iv, 1.

Poet.—

The vacant leaves thy mind's Imprint will bear,

And of this book this learning may'st thou taste.—*Sonnet 77*.

Note.—In this metaphor our bard shows his intimacy with the compositor's problem, in "making-up" for press. Columns of text divide up, and leave an awkward bit over, that cannot be omitted, or squeezed into the final sheet. So a supplemental last sheet carries this bit of overplus matter, with several blank pages, one of which will bear the colophon or imprint. To the compositor, paid at so much per sheet, these blanks were known colloquially as "Fat," for they earned equal pay with type-filled leaves.

Prospero.—
And ye, that on the sands with Printless foot,
Do chase the ebbing Neptune . . .
—*The Tempest*, v, 1.

Marcus.—Heaven guide thy pen to Print thy sorrows plain.—*Titus Andronicus*, iv, 1.

Speed.—All this I speak in Print, for in Print I found it.—*Two Gentlemen*, ii, 1.

Poet.—
His tenderer cheek receives her soft hand's Print . . .
Pure lips, sweet seals, on my soft lips Imprinted.
—*Venus and Adonis*, lines 353 and 511.

Paulina.—
Behold, my lords, although the Print be little,
The whole matter and copy of the father. . .
The very mould and frame of hand, nail, finger . . .—*Winter's Tale*, ii, 3.

Note.—Any printer setting up the second edition of a book in smaller type and size will recognize the typographical reminiscence and accuracy herein. It is scarcely conceivable that a few brief lines, bearing five distinct typographical words, three of them technical, should proceed from anyone's brain unfamiliar with printing.

Leontes.—
Your mother was most true to wedlock, Prince,
For she did Print your royal father off . . .
—*Winter's Tale*, v, 1.

Note.—What more natural simile for a printer-poet to use, or one more appropriate for the audience to hear? The printer's daily experience of exact agreement between type-face and impression must have suggested the image.

PRIVILEGE OR SOLE RIGHT. *See* PRESS.

PROOFS

Caius Lucius.—Let Proof Speak.—*Cymbeline*, iii, 1.

Duke of Buckingham.—Proofs as clear as founts in July.—*King Henry VIII*, i, 1.

Duke.—Nay, if the Devil hath given thee Proofs for sin, thou wilt prove his.—*Measure for Measure*, iii, 2.

PUBLISHING

Steward.—We wound our modesty, and make foul the clearness of our deservings, when of ourselves we publish them.—*All's Well*, i, 3.

Cymbeline.—Publish we this peace to all our subjects.—*Cymbeline*, v, 5.

Archbishop of York.—Let us on, and Publish the occasion of our arms.—2 *King Henry IV*, i, 3.

King Henry.—If he be guilty, as 'tis Published . . .—2 *King Henry VI*, iii, 2.

King Lear.—A constant will to Publish our daughters' several dowers.—*King Lear*, i, 1.

Oswald.—Wherefore, bold peasant, darest thou support a Published traitor?—*King Lear*, iv, 6.

Poet.—
Why is Collatine the Publisher of that rich jewel? . . .
And so to Publish Tarquin's foul offence.
—*Lucrece*, lines 33 and 1852.

Clerk (Nerissa).—Whose trial shall better Publish his commendation. — *Merchant of Venice*, iv, 1.

Friar.—And Publish it, that she is dead indeed.—*Much Ado*, iv, 1.

Poet.—Whose rich esteeming, the owner's tongue doth Publish everywhere.—*Sonnet* 102.

Tranio.—Hath Published and proclaimed it openly.—*Taming of Shrew*, iv, 2.

Painter.—When comes your book forth?

Poet.—Upon the heels of my presentment, sir. *Timon of Athens*, i, 1.

Nestor.—In the Publication, make no strain.—*Troilus and Cressida*, i, 3.   . . .

Thersites.—A proof of strength she could not Publish more . . .

Troilus.—Shall I not lie in Publishing a truth?—*Troilus and Cressida*, v, 2.

Sebastian.—Yet thus far I will boldly Publish her.—*Twelfth Night*, ii, 1.

Proteus.—Hath made me Publisher of this pretence.—*Two Gentlemen*, iii, 1.

Hermione.—How will this grieve you, when you shall come to clearer knowledge, that you thus have Published me.—*Winter's Tale*, ii, 1.

QUAD

Iago.—I have rubbed this young Quat almost to the sense.—*Othello*, v, 1.

Note.—As a small or trifling thing, Shakespeare may have had a Quad in mind at that moment.

READING

Rosalind.—I have heard him Read many lectures against it.—*As You Like It*, iii, 2.

Menenius.—I have been the Book of his good Acts, whence men have Read his fame unparalleled; haply amplified.—*Coriolanus*, v, 2.

Caesar.—He Reads much; he is a great observer; and he looks quite through the deeds of men; he loves no Plays, as thou dost, Antony . . .—*Julius Caesar*, i, 2.

King Henry.—Proclaimed at market-crosses: Read in churches.—1 *King Henry IV*, v, 1.

King Ferdinand.—How well he is Read, to reason against Reading.—*Love's Labours*, i, 1.

Angelo—Like a good thing, being often Read, grown seared and tedious.—*Measure for Measure*, ii, 4.

Duke.—If I Read it not truly, my ancient skill beguiles me.—*Measure for Measure*, iv, 2.

Mrs. Ford.—We burn daylight; here, Read, Read.—*Merry Wives*, ii, 1.

Servant.—Can you Read anything you see?

Romeo.—Ay, if I know the letters and the language.—*Romeo and Juliet*, i, 2.

Gremio.—See you Read no other lectures to her.—*Taming of Shrew*, i, 2.

Malvolio.—I will Read politic authors.—*Twelfth Night*, ii, 5.

See also—BIBLE, BINDING, BOOKS, LEARNING, LIBRARY, VOLUME.

REGISTER

Enobarbus.—

But let the world rank me in Register
A Master-Leaver and a future . . .
    —*Antony and Cleopatra*, iv, 9.

Note.—In this reference Shakespeare recalls the skill and practice required to machine each side of the sheet, so that the lines of matter back each other precisely. The accuracy of sight and touch had not escaped his lynx eyes.

REVIEWING

Poet.—When thou Reviewest this, thou dost Review the very part . . .—*Sonnet 74*.

Camillo.—In whose company I shall Review Sicilia.—*Winter's Tale*, iv, 4.

RHYMES

Cleopatra.—And scald Rhymers ballad us out of tune.—*Antony and Cleopatra*, v, 2.

Biron.—Regent of Love-Rhymes, lord of folded arms.—*Love's Labours*, iii, 1.

SALE. *See* SELLING.

SCHEDULE

Artemidorus.—Hail, Caesar! Read this Schedule.—*Julius Caesar*, iii, 1.

Archbishop of York.—This Schedule . . . contains our general grievances.—2 *King Henry IV*, iv, 1.

King Ferdinand.—To keep those statutes that are recorded in this Schedule here . . . —*Love's Labours*, i, 1.

Poet.—

By this short Schedule, Collatine may know
Her grief, but not her grief's true quality.
            —*Lucrece*, line 1312.

Prince of Arragon.—What's here? The portrait of a blinking idiot. Presenting me a Schedule. I will read it.—*Merchant of Venice*, ii, 9.

Olivia.—I will give out divers Schedules of my beauty. It shall be inventoried.—*Twelfth Night*, i, 5.

SCRIBE

Enobarbus.—Hearts, tongues, figures, Scribes, bards, poets, cannot Think, speak, cast, write, sing, number, ho!—*Antony and Cleopatra*, iii, 2.

Chiron.—And if thy stumps will let thee, play the Scribe.—*Titus Andronicus*, ii, 5.

Speed.—That my master, being Scribe, to himself should write the letter.—*Two Gentlemen*, ii, 1.

SCRIP

Touchstone.—Though not with bag and baggage, yet with Scrip and Scrippage.—*As You Like It*, iii, 2.

Bottom.—Call them generally, man by man, according to the Scrip.—*Midsummer Night's Dream*, i, 2.

SCRIVENER

Tranio.—My boy shall fetch the Scrivener presently.—*Taming of Shrew*, iv, 4.

SCROLL

Octavius Caesar.—Do not exceed the prescript of the Scroll.—*Antony and Cleopatra*, iii, 8.

Poet.—With a steadfast eye receives the Scroll, without a "yea" or "no" . . .—*Lucrece*, line 1340.

Demetrius.—What's here? A Scroll, and written round about . . .—*Titus Andronicus*, iv, 2.

SELLING

Rosalind.—Sell when you can: you are not for all markets.—*As You Like It*, iii, 5.

Cloten.—There is gold for you; Sell me your good report.—*Cymbeline*, ii, 3.

Princess.—Not uttered by base Sale of chapmen's tongues.—*Love's Labours*, ii, 1.

Costard.—I will never buy and Sell out of this word.—*Love's Labours*, iii, 1.

Biron.—
To things of Sale a Seller's praise belongs . . .
And we that Sell by gross, the Lord doth know
Have not the grace to grace it with such show.—*Love's Labours*, iv, 3, and v, 2.

Lady Macduff's son.—Then you'll buy them to Sell again.—*Macbeth*, iv, 2.

Shylock.—I will buy with you; Sell with you . . .—*Merchant of Venice*, i, 3.

Poet.—Sold cheap what is most dear . . .—*Sonnet* 110.

Thersites.—And thou art bought and Sold among those of any wit.—*Troilus and Cressida*, ii, 1.

Paris.—
Fair Diomed, you do as chapmen do
Dispraise the thing that you desire to buy
But we in silence hold this virtue well
We'll not commend what we desire to Sell.
—*Troilus and Cressida*, iv, 1.

Florizel.—When you sing, I'd have you buy and Sell so.—*Winter's Tale*, iv, 3.

SENECA

Polonius.—Seneca cannot be too heavy, nor Plautus too light.—*Hamlet*, ii, 2.

Note.—Between 1516 and 1634 no fewer than twenty-two different editions of Seneca's Tragedies and other pieces appeared from English presses.

SEWING. *See* STITCHING.

SHANK

Jaques.—
His youthful hose, well saved,
A world too wide for his shrunk Shank.
—*As You Like It*, ii, 7.

Note.—Under the Tudor system, of making type in hand moulds, a proportion of all the castings was imperfect. Until the mould became warm by use, the liquid metal solidified too soon, and thus the body, or shank, of the type was shrunk. So we find this apposite allusion to type shanks and leg shanks.

SHEET

Princess.—As much love in rhyme as would be crammed up in a Sheet of paper.—*Love's Labours*, v, 2.

Claudio.—Now you talk of a Sheet of paper, I remember a pretty jest.—*Much Ado*, ii, 3.

Sir Toby.—
As many lies as will lie in thy Sheet of paper,
Although the Sheet were big enough for the Bed of Ware in England.
—*Twelfth Night*, iii, 2.

SHOP

Cloten.—Therein I must play the Workman.—*Cymbeline*, iv, 1.

Fool.—Learn more than thou trowest.—*King Lear*, i, 4.

Poet.—
To find where your true image pictured lies
Which in my bosom's Shop is hanging still
That hath his windows glazed with thine eyes . . .—*Sonnet* 24.

See also—BUYING.

See also—SELLING.

SLICE

Nym.—
Slice! I say; pauca, pauca,
Slice!—that's my humour.
—*Merry Wives*, i, 1.

Note.—Maybe a remembrance of the printer's flat knife, called a Slice, for spreading ink.

SOCRATES

Petrucio.—As curst and shrewd as Socrates' Xantippe.—*Taming of Shrew,* i, 2.

Note.—Socrates, the "wisest of men," was born and lived at Athens, 469 to 399 B.C. His whole life, according to Xenophon, passed in doing good, and nothing wrong. Yet, like Jesus Christ later, he succeeded in making enemies, and was innocent when condemned to death. No edition of his writings appeared in England before our poet's death, but the Latin epitaph on Shakespeare's tomb compares him with Socrates, Nestor, and Virgil.

SONNET

First Lord.—Will you give me a copy of the Sonnet you writ to Diana.—*All's Well,* iv, 3.

Dauphin.—I once writ a Sonnet in his praise, and began thus: "Wonder of nature . . ." —*King Henry V,* iii, 7.

Biron.—She hath one of my Sonnets already. —*Love's Labours,* iv, 3.

Margaret.—Will you then write me a Sonnet in praise of my beauty.—*Much Ado,* v, 2.

Claudio.—

Here's a paper written in his hand,
A halting Sonnet of his own pure brain.
                —*Much Ado,* v, 4.

See also—POESY.

SOUTHWELL

Bolingbroke.—John Southwell, read you; and let us to our work.—2 *King Henry VI,* i, 4.

Romeo.—Transparent heretics; be burnt for liars.—*Romeo and Juliet,* i. 2.

Note.—The use by Shakespeare of the surname of Southwell, as a priest, is curious, seeing that a few years earlier, Robert Southwell, a Roman priest and poet, had been tortured and executed at Tyburn. His volumes of verse exhibit high merit.

STAMPING

Cominius.—His sword, death's Stamp; where it did mark, it took.—*Coriolanus,* ii. 2.

King Lear.—Let it Stamp wrinkles in her brow. —*King Lear,* i, 4.

Fenton.—Yet, wooing thee, I found thee of more value than Stamps in gold.—*Merry Wives,* iii, 4.

Note.—During the fifteenth and sixteenth centuries, it was a common custom, among leading bookbinders, in England and over-sea, to use engraved blocks, of decorative or pictorial pattern; these blocks covered the sides of a book, either partly or wholly, in "blind" relief, or in gold, and such bindings are called "Stamped."

STITCHING

Valeria.—What are you Stitching here? Come, lay aside your Stitchery.—*Coriolanus,* i, 3.

Othello.—In her prophetic fury, Sewed the work.—*Othello,* iii, 4.

Maria.—If you desire the spleen, and will laugh yourself into Stitches . . .—*Twelfth Night,* iii, 2.

SUPERSCRIPTION

Duke of Gloster.—Doth this churlish Superscription pretend some alteration in good will?—1 *King Henry VI,* iv, 1.

Holofernes.—I will over-glance the Superscript. —*Love's Labours,* iv, 2.

Page.—Read me the Superscription of these letters—*Timon of Athens,* ii, 2.

SUPERVISION

Hamlet.—On the Supervise, no leisure bated. —*Hamlet,* v, 2.

Holofernes.—Let me Supervise the canzonet. —*Love's Labours,* iv, 2.

Iago.—Would you, the Supervisor, grossly gape on?—*Othello,* iii, 3.

TEREUS

Iachimo.—

She hath been reading late the "Tale of Tereus"
Here the leaf is turned down, where Philomel gave up.—*Cymbeline,* ii, 2.

Poet.—

Fie, fie, fie, now would she cry;
Tereu, Tereu! by and by.
                —*Passionate Pilgrim,* line 386.

Titus.—

. . . Lavinia, shall I read?
This is the tragic "Tale of Philomel"
And treats of Tereus' treason and his rape.
                —*Titus Andronicus,* iv, 1.

Note.—The "Tale of Tereus" is the appalling tragedy of Philomela, daughter of Pandion, King of Athens. Her outrage and mutilation formed a basis for our poet's plot of "Titus Andronicus." The ancient legend relates how Philomela, to escape the fury of Tereus, was changed into a nightingale, while her sister Progne became a swallow. Shakespeare would be able to read the story, among many other classical legends, in Ælianus. "Registre of hystories. Deliuered in Englishe by Abraham Fleming . . . 1576." Two copies only are known; one at the British Museum, and one in my collection. Shakespeare twice refers to Philomel's sorrow in "Lucrece." In the "Passionate Pilgrim" printed by Wm. Jaggard in 1599, 1604, and 1612, our poet adopts the tradition, cited by Ælianus, that the nightingale leans his breast "up-till a thorn" when reciting that characteristic note, long, low, and emotional, in his midnight carol.

TEXT

Katherine.—Fair as a Text "B" in a copy-book. —*Love's Labours,* v, 2.

THUCYDIDES

Canidius.—Toward Peloponnesus are they fled. —*Antony and Cleopatra,* iii, 8.

Note.—Thucydides himself is not named in Shakespeare, but our bard had probably read his folio "Hystory of the Peloponnesian warre" which came out in 1550, and was again issued in folio by W. Jaggard in 1607.

TITLE

Northumberland.—This man's brow, like to a Title-leaf.—2 *King Henry IV,* i, 1.

Simonides.—To place upon the volume of your deeds, as in a Title-page.—*Pericles,* ii, 3.

TRANSPOSING

Malcolm.—That which you are, my thoughts cannot Transpose.—*Macbeth,* iv, 3.

Helena.—
Things base and vile, holding no quantity,
Love can Transpose to form and dignity.
—*Midsummer Night's Dream,* i, 1.

TRIMMING

Iago.—Trimmed in forms and visages of duty. —*Othello,* i, 1.

Poet.—And needy nothing Trimmed in jollity. —*Sonnet 66.*

TYPE

Richard of York.—Thy father bears the Type of King of Naples.—3 *King Henry VI,* i, 4.

King Richard.—The high imperial Type of this earth's glory.—*King Richard III,* iv, 4.

Poet.—
O, no! that cannot be
Of that true Type hath Tarquin rifled me.
—*Lucrece,* line 1050.

See also—APOSTROPHE, CHARACTERS, COMMA, COMPOSITION, EXCLAMATION, FIGURES, INDENT, LETTERS, LOCKING-UP, METAL, MOULDING, NONPAREIL, OVER-SET, PERIOD, POINTS, SHANK.

VELLUM. *See* PARCHMENT.

VERSE. *See* BALLAD, BOOK OF SONGS, ODE, POESY, POET, PRICK-SONG, RHYMES, SONNET.

VIRGIL

Antony.—Dido and her Æneas shall want troops . . .—*Antony and Cleopatra,* iv, 12.

Hamlet.—'Twas Æneas' tale to Dido, and thereabout of it especially where he speaks of Priam's slaughter.—*Hamlet,* ii, 2.

Note.—Though Virgil is not actually named, his "Dido and Æneas" poem is quoted several times by Shakespeare. From 1490 to 1638 forty-eight separate issues of Virgil passed through English presses, proving Virgil's continuous popularity.

VOLUME

Coriolanus.—That, for the poorest piece, will bear the knave by the Volume.—*Coriolanus,* iii, 2.

Imogen.—In the world's Volume, our Britain seems as of it, but not in it.—*Cymbeline,* iii, 4.

Hamlet.—Within the book and Volume of my brain.—*Hamlet,* i, 5.

Suffolk.—
Had I sufficient skill to utter them
Would make a Volume of enticing lines
Able to ravish any dull conceit.
—1 *King Henry VI,* v, 5.

Northumberland.—Foretells the nature of a tragic Volume.—2 *King Henry IV,* i, 1.

King Philip.—And the hand of time shall draw this brief into as huge a Volume.— *King John,* ii, 1.

Aumerle.—He should have had a Volume of farewells.—*King Richard II,* i, 4.

Armado.—Devise, wit; write, pen; for I am for whole Volumes in folio.—*Love's Labours,* i, 2.

Old Man.—Within the Volume of which time I have seen hours dreadful, and things strange.—*Macbeth,* ii, 4.

Duke.—Volumes of report . . . upon thy doings.—*Measure for Measure,* iv, 1.

Lady Capulet.—

Read o'er the Volume of young Paris' face,
And find delight writ there with beauty's
  pen . . .
And what, obscured, in this fair Volume
  lies . . . . —*Romeo and Juliet,* i, 3.

Prospero.—With Volumes that I prize above my dukedom.—*The Tempest,* i, 2.

Nestor.—To their subsequent Volumes . . .
  —*Troilus and Cressida,* i, 3.

WIT

Biron.—

This fellow pecks up Wit, as pigeons peas,
And utters it again when God doth please;
He is Wit's pedlar, and retails his wares
At wakes and wassails, meetings, markets,
  fairs.—*Love's Labours,* v, 2.

See also—HUNDRED MERRY TALES.

WORM-HOLES

Duke of Exeter.—

'Tis no sinister, nor no awkward claim,
Picked from the Worm-holes of long-
  vanished days
Nor from the dust of old oblivion raked . . .
  —*King Henry V,* ii, 4.

POET.—To fill with Worm-holes, stately monuments.—*Lucrece,* line 946.

Note.—Our common foe, the book-moth (near relative of the clothes-moth and wood-moth) when in the grub, or larva, state, plays havoc with old books, and is commonly known as the "book-worm." Its depredations appear to have been familiar to our poet. A chapter is devoted to book-worms by Wm. Blades in his entertaining work, the "Enemies of Books," with illustrations. There are several varieties of the grub, which feed on the paste attaching end-papers to covers, and also on wheat.

WRITING

Hamlet.—The story is extant, and Writ in choice Italian.—*Hamlet,* iii, 2.

Chorus.—

Thus far with rough and all un-able pen,
Our bending Author hath pursued the story.
  —*King Henry V,* Epilogue.

Earl of Suffolk.—I'll call for pen and ink, and Write my mind.—1 *King Henry VI,* v, 3.

Gloster.—

Had he a hand to Write this?
A heart and brain to breed it in?
  —*King Lear,* i, 2.

Poet.—

Nor read the subtle-shining secrecies,
Writ in the glassy margents of such books.
  —*Lucrece,* line 102.

Theseus.—The Poet's pen turns them to shapes.
  —*Midsummer Night's Dream,* v, 1.

Valentine.—I Writ at random, very doubtfully.

Silvia.—Yes, yes; the lines are very quaintly Writ.—*Two Gentlemen,* ii, 1.

Chorus.—Not in confidence of Author's pen, or Actor's voice.—*Troilus and Cressida,* Prologue.

XENOPHON

Countess.—

I shall as famous be, by this exploit,
As Scythian Tomyris by Cyrus' death.
  —1 *King Henry VI,* ii, 3.

Note.—Though not expressly named, Xenophon must have been very well known to all bookmen and writers of the sixteenth century, for his works were issued in eleven editions between 1532 and 1632, in England, especially his "Life of Cyrus."

YELLOWING

Poet.—So should my papers, Yellowed with their age, be scorned.—*Sonnet* 17.

Macbeth.—My way of life is fallen into the sere, the Yellow leaf . . .—*Macbeth,* v, 3.

Note.—Our poet here recalls manuscripts, exposed to sun or strong light, and so become faded. He probably handled such, while correcting for the press.

*   *   *

The foregoing "Alphabet" reveals that among the ancient classics, not expressly named by Shakespeare, are these—

Aristophanes.—Only one play of his appeared in English, ere Shakespeare's death, "The Knights . . . Oxford, 1593."

IMPRESSIO LIBRORVM.

Potest vt vna vox capi aure plurima: Linunt ita vna scripta mille paginas.

Tudor Printery, circa 1585.
For processes depicted, see Francis Quarles' verse, page 30.

Bookstore and Printery for four hundred years.

Owned and directed by John and Elizabeth Jaggard from 1594 to 1648.

No. 7 Fleet Street, at the " Signe of the Hande and Starre," just before demolition in 1907.

Dick's famous Coffee House, adjoining, was once John Jaggard's Printery.

Claudian.—No issue before 1617.

Demosthenes.—Four English editions came out, between 1570 and 1597.

Euripides.—Not a single English printing, before our poet's end.

Herodotus.—Two editions were published, in 1584 and 1591.

Justinian.—No English edition appeared before 1640.

Livy.—Three issues appeared in London, in 1589 and 1600.

Plato.—One issue only, London 1604.

Pliny.—Six English versions were published between 1566 and 1635.

Sallust.—From 1520 to 1615 five editions in England appeared.

Sophocles.—Like Aristophanes, only one play of this dramatist came out in England; his "Antigone" in 1581.

Terence.—In striking contrast to the foregoing, no fewer than twenty-four English editions appeared of this dramatist, between 1483 and 1629.

* * *

That completes my case. It only remains for discerning "Members of the Jury" to consider the evidence adduced, and arrive at a verdict.

Pisanio.—Then, sir, this Paper is the history of my knowledge.—*Cymbeline,* iii, 5.

Dauphin of France.—It is a theme as fluent as the sea, . . . 'tis a subject for a Sovereign to reason on; and for the world, familiar to us, and unknown,—to lay apart their particular functions, and wonder at him.—*King Henry V,* iii, 7.

Before adding my "Summary," an idea, perhaps apropos to the occasion, arises. Since William the Norman conquered Britain, several others, all yclept William, have done a little conquering. It might be well to briefly record their names, dates, and doings, on a "Scroll of Fame," printed on vellum, and glazed, to hang in Stationers' Hall. This, firstly, to show foreigners we are not ashamed of our past, and, secondly, to encourage our future generations. Those rendering permanent literary service should be eligible for that proud Scroll. To begin with, as a tentative suggestion list, seven men spring to mind, all named William, whose claims seem patent:—

William Caxton, 1422-91.—Author, translator, linguist, and first British printer.

William Tyndale, 1500-36.—Scholar, tutor, refugee, first English Bible translator, strangled and burnt at the stake. His last prayer, "Lord, open England's eyes."

William Shakespeare, 1564-1616. — Printer, bookman, player, playhouse shareholder, landowner, England's national poet, and the world's leading dramatist.

William Jaggard, 1567-1623.—Scholar, translator, printer, engraver, pioneer publisher, editor, bibliographer, friend of Shakespeare, and sponsor of his first edition of 1623.

William Thomas Lowndes, 1798-1843.—Son and grandson of booksellers, scholar, pioneer bibliographer. Health broken, and mind deranged, by life of drudgery and poverty.

William Blades, 1824-90.—Scholar, author, printer, bibliographer, printer's benefactor.

William Carew Hazlitt, 1834-1913.—Scholar, bibliographer, author, numismatist, one of four generations of literary celebrities.

As Ulysses says (*Troilus and Cressida,* iii, 3): "Time hath, my lord, a wallet at his back." So let us close with the Summary, or "Seven Ages" of a Printer found in Francis Quarles' "Divine Fancies . . . 1632." Like many others, Quarles seems to have drawn inspiration from Shakespeare's Jaques in "As You Like It"—

The World's a Printing House: Our
  Words, Our Thoughts,
Our Deeds, are Characters of several sizes.
Each Soule is a Compositor; of whose
  Faults
The Levits [Levers] are Correctors:
  Heaven Revises:
Death is the common Press; from whence,
  being driven,
We are Gathered, Sheet by Sheet, and
  Bound for Heaven.

*   *   *

THE CHAIRMAN, in opening the discussion, said that Captain Jaggard's strongest points, in his argument that Shakespeare was a printer, were the number of references to the technical printing terms used by Shakespeare; at the same time, he did not quite follow how it was that all the classics, referred to, showed that Shakespeare was a printer and not a scholar.

J. G. WILSON asked the lecturer if he could state whether his interpretation of the line in *Macbeth* of "the sere, the Yellow leaf" was one that had been suggested before. Strangely enough, he (the speaker) had been asked the question only the previous day. The lecturer's explanation of the term was most illuminating.

THE LECTURER replied that in this instance he had put in the example because there was just a doubt: the term might apply to a yellow, sere or wrinkled, crooked old leaf, off a tree, or it might just as well apply to an old, wrinkled, crooked leaf out of a book. It could be read either way, but he thought the preponderance of opinion would be that it meant a leaf off a tree. However, he had put it in because either interpretation was arguable. A lawyer would certainly bring it in if he were arguing the case.

J. G. WILSON thought the lecturer's explanation was well founded, and it was in his favour that the line was always misquoted; it was one of the most misquoted lines of Shakespeare. It was always quoted as "the sere *and* yellow leaf." The correct quotation, "The sere, the Yellow leaf," would indicate that it was something in the nature of a sheet of paper.

THE LECTURER, in reply to the chairman's opening question, said his introduction of the classics was in order to show Shakespeare's connection with the book trade and his familiarity with editions and contents of the ancient classics of the sixteenth century, which would be on sale in the various bookshops, and no doubt in the bookshop in which Shakespeare assisted. It was also to show how familiar Shakespeare was with the writings of at least eighteen of the classics. There were only about twelve out of perhaps thirty that he had omitted to name. The reference to classics did not connect up with printing so strongly as with Shakespeare's experience with books and the book trade. He (the lecturer) was trying to develop Mr. Blades's idea and to show that Shakespeare was more than a printer— that he was also a book-man; indeed, it was his conviction that Shakespeare was a book-man.

A. GOMME asked if the lecturer had any theory as to why Shakespeare had left the printing trade and taken up the theatre?

THE LECTURER replied that he had a theory, but it was only a theory; he had not a scrap of evidence to support it, except that the change-over had certainly taken place soon after 1590. He thought that Shakespeare's leaning towards the drama had always been with him; in fact, it had been born in him. He must have started, as a youth, writing verse, and it

30

took the dramatic form when he reached London. When he got to London his pen and brain would be always at work in some capacity, and he must have seen the opportunity and scope there were for a new style of drama; for it must never be forgotten that Shakespeare was the founder of our English school of drama at that point. Practically the old style of drama had depended on the ancient dry classical school, with precious little everyday humanity or humour in it. Shakespeare then came and brought a new idea altogether. He made his plays describe everyday men and women, and everyday life, and he introduced so much humour into them that they were made attractive to everybody. He had seen the opportunity, and he started by polishing up other people's plays and then finally launched out on his own account. That was his (the lecturer's) theory, but he had no evidence in support of it.

THE CHAIRMAN said the lecturer had spoken of Shakespeare polishing up other people's plays. The well-known Shakespearean scholar, Mr. J. M. Robertson, had suggested that some of the plays were composed by contemporary dramatists such as Kyd and Marlowe, and then written up by Shakespeare. It was interesting to note that Richard Simpson published in 1872 a book, called "The School of Shakespeare," in which he drew attention to the fact that there was an anonymous play, called "Sir Thomas More," which contained certain passages apparently written by Shakespeare. When the original manuscript came to be examined a few years ago, it was found that those particular passages were written in a different hand, and scholars now agree that this is the only

example of Shakespeare's handwriting—apart from his signatures—in existence. Was there anything in the theory that the plays had been written by contemporary dramatists and that Shakespeare had finished them off?

THE LECTURER replied that, in addition to what was called "The Canon of Shakespeare"—that was to say, the thirty-seven accepted plays and the three main poems—there were about sixteen other plays in which somebody had had either a finger or a hand; that was to say, somebody else had written a play and had brought it to Shakespeare, knowing Shakespeare's ability, to knock off the rough corners and to polish it up. Those plays were being reprinted over and over again as "The Shakespeare Apocrypha," in which here and there could be seen the unmistakable touch of Shakespeare; but the construction generally was weak and poor. Personally, he was a firm believer in Shakespeare's collaboration in the play of "Sir Thomas More," and he was a firm supporter of the authenticity and genuineness of Shakespeare's handwriting appearing therein, because some years ago he had taken a great deal of trouble, going into the question of Shakespeare's handwriting, and he was convinced that the example quoted by the chairman was really the handwriting of Shakespeare.

In addition to these sixteen attributed plays, there were two, "Cardenio," and another, of the text of which all trace had disappeared. Two others, entitled "Double Falsehood" and "Vortigern," ascribed to Shakespeare long after his death, proved to be impudent forgeries.

WILLIAM POEL, in proposing a hearty vote of thanks to the lecturer, said he had no business in the room at all; he had really come to the meeting thinking he would be entering a theatre, instead of which he found he had come into a book-shop!

He (the speaker) had spent much of his life in telling people that, unless they could speak the words of Shakespeare intelligently and with a sense of rhyme and rhythm, they were not interpreting Shakespeare, or getting the spectators to be interested in what was the greatest thing in connection with his art—namely, his unparalleled language.

He thought the question was easily answered as to why Shakespeare had started to write plays. Shakespeare became a writer of plays because he wanted money and wanted it quickly. His father and mother had inherited a very valuable estate of sixty acres in Stratford-on-Avon, together with dwellings and farm buildings. They were landed property people; they were well off. However, all that went, and with it disappeared the young Shakespeare, who very wisely set off for London in search of remunerative work. But why tradition should have said that he walked there "on his feet," no one yet has been able to explain! For all he had to do was to go into his father's stables, get one of the farm horses, and ride off—no doubt selling the horse on his arrival in the city, a custom not unusual in those days. And in this we find the probable explanation why the lad was not apprenticed to any trade; he was to be a landed proprietor—so it was presumed. When Ann, therefore, married Shakespeare, she thought she had found a husband who had sixty acres coming to him at his parents' death, besides a comfortable home. This disappointment seems to have made a lasting feud between the two families, as Shakespeare had to learn to his cost.

Then arises the question—how did the young man become connected with the theatre? The poet Pope gives the answer in expressing his opinion that Shakespeare wrote plays "for gain and not for fame," which is true but not the whole truth. For if the dramatist had been an indifferent actor, like Ben Jonson, he would have died a poor man even if he had written—including poems—twice forty plays. Jonson, that is, failing as a player, the Globe players would not take him as a shareholder, while Shakespeare, on the stage, was the delight of both actors and audience.

So Shakespeare became a dramatist, not because he had wanted to write for the stage—he disliked the stage; he believed it was lowering to him—but because he wanted money. The poet had a net, and into that net he threw everything. It is doubtful, indeed, if anyone had done less original work for the theatre than he. Here was Marlowe writing a play in the theatre, and there was Shakespeare; and both men drew their work from various sources.

He (Mr. Poel) asked the audience present to think of what they had heard that night—a fact which should be remembered, namely, the industry and brainwork entailed in collecting all these things which they had heard that Shakespeare had put into his plays.

In the Folio there were thirty-six plays which were called Shakespeare's, and they were regarded as such because his fellow actors had acted in them; but as to seven of those plays, all men of letters and experts were agreed in saying that very little only of them was of Shakespeare's writing. Nor had he taken the trouble even to plan the action of any. He (Mr. Poel) asked anyone to take up their Gervinus, the great critic of Shakespeare, and to read what he said of these seven plays. "Either Shakespeare's mind must have gone wrong, or he must have been very ill." Yet these seven plays, of which parts attributed to the dramatist were of small account, appear in the First Folio. Let them be removed! They never ought to have gone into it.

JOHN G. WILSON, in seconding the vote of thanks, remarked that Captain Jaggard went back in name and tradition to that great man William Jaggard who had printed that most wonderful book in the world—the Folio Shakespeare—in 1623. He congratulated printers on the fact that Captain Jaggard had proved that Shakespeare was a printer; but, as a bookseller himself, he wanted to share in that honour because it seemed that Shakespeare had been also a bookseller—in fact, he rather thought that it had been in his capacity as a bookseller that Shakespeare had gained all the knowledge that he was able to put into his plays.

Captain Jaggard had filled in a rather mysterious period in Shakespeare's life, but there was another period in that great man's life which also gave rise to speculation. Shakespeare had been at the very height of his power in 1609 (when he had written "The Tempest") when, it was believed, he had left London and had gone to Stratford-on-Avon. Shakespeare had not died until 1616. What had Shakespeare been doing at the height of his tremendous powers between 1609 and 1616? Would it be fanciful of him (Mr. Wilson) to suggest that Shakespeare had gone to Stratford in order to open a private printing press, and that he had printed there himself all the great poetry that he was writing at that time, and that one of these fine days Mr. Hodgson would find a copy of such work and sell it for £50,000?

The vote of thanks was carried by acclamation.

THE LECTURER, in acknowledging the vote, said he could only wish that time had been long enough to go into the subject at greater length. It was an enormous subject with immense ramifications, and was capable of a most interesting debate.

Mr. Wilson had asked what Shakespeare was doing from 1610 to 1616 when he had been at the height of his powers. He was writing plays. "The Tempest" had been most certainly written at Stratford-on-Avon, for the simple reason that until 1609 the account of the great storm in the Bermudas had not been printed. It had been printed only in 1609, and supposing that Shakespeare had got a copy at once it would have taken him a little time to have composed that magnificent play. It was also believed that he wrote "King Henry VIII," "Cymbeline," and "Winter's Tale" there. Then came the breakdown in health, Shakespeare became ill, and, if anyone wanted an account of Shakespeare's condition at that time, he had only to read Dr. J. F. Nisbet's book, "The Insanity of Genius." Not only did genius not carry on, but the race itself died out. Shakespeare's own direct race died out in the second generation. When Nature worked up to fruition, or the splendid flower, as it did in Shakespeare, it exhausted itself. Shakespeare became very ill at Stratford-on-Avon from either paralysis or heart trouble, and it was to be assumed that he had gone on working until he could work no longer; he had worn himself out with hard work. One could hardly imagine the power, the mental toil, and the knowledge that were required to write his plays.

Mr. Poel had suggested that there were seven plays in the Folio which had precious little of Shakespeare about them, but might he (the lecturer) say that there was a delightful little piece of Shakespeare which would not be found in any edition of his writings, but which could be found, with its source, at pages 170-171 of his (the lecturer's) "Bibliography," as follows:

> Crowns have their compass,
>   Lengths of days their date,
> Triumphs their tombs,
>   Felicity its fate—
> Of more than earth can Earth
>   Make none partaker,
> But knowledge makes the King
>   Most like his Maker.

The lecturer then proposed a hearty vote of thanks to Mr. Hodgson for having taken the chair, which was carried with acclamation, and the meeting terminated.